PENGUIN BOOKS

HOW TO SURVIVE HISTORY

Cody Cassidy is the author of *Who Ate the First Oyster?* and coauthor of *And Then You're Dead*. His writing has appeared in *Wired* and *Slate,* among many other publications. He lives in San Francisco.

ALSO BY CODY CASSIDY

Who Ate the First Oyster?
And Then You're Dead

HOW TO SURVIVE
HISTORY

How to Outrun a **Tyrannosaurus**,
Escape **Pompeii**, Get Off the *Titanic*,
and Survive the Rest of History's
Deadliest Catastrophes

Cody Cassidy

PENGUIN BOOKS

PENGUIN BOOKS
An imprint of Penguin Random House LLC
penguinrandomhouse.com

Illustrations by Cody Cassidy and Kevin Plottner

The chapters "The Dinosaur Age," "The Chicxulub Asteroid," "Pompeii," "The Donner Party," "The Sinking of the *Titanic*," and "The Worst Tornado in American History" originally appeared, in different forms, in *Wired* in 2020–2021.

LIBRARY OF CONGRESS CATALOGING-IN-PUBLICATION DATA
Names: Cassidy, Cody, author.
Title: How to survive history : how to outrun a Tyrannosaurus, escape Pompeii, get off the Titanic, and survive the rest of history's deadliest catastrophes / Cody Cassidy.
Description: [New York, NY] : Penguin Books, [2023] |
Includes bibliographical references.
Identifiers: LCCN 2022051160 (print) | LCCN 2022051161 (ebook) |
ISBN 9780143136408 (trade paperback) | ISBN 9780525507932 (ebook)
Subjects: LCSH: Disasters—History. | Survival. | History—Miscellanea.
Classification: LCC D24 .C315 2023 (print) |
LCC D24 (ebook) | DDC 904—dc23/eng/20230111
LC record available at https://lccn.loc.gov/2022051160
LC ebook record available at https://lccn.loc.gov/2022051161

Printed in the United States of America
5th Printing

Set in Charter
Designed by Sabrina Bowers

For Mom and Dad

CONTENTS

INTRODUCTION

A few years ago I read a study written by a team of paleontologists that seemed to suggest I could outrun the most powerful predator in the history of our planet.

I found this surprising.

I consider myself a mediocre example of an athletically pedestrian species, with a top speed well below that of nearly every predator, never mind the deadliest. Yet the evidence that I could outsprint the formidable *Tyrannosaurus rex* appeared convincing. By measuring the size, musculature, balance, bone strength, and stride length of the great saurian, along with the application of an obscure formula originally developed to design boat hulls and ingeniously repurposed to determine running speeds, these paleontologists produced an estimation of the *T. rex*'s top speed that appeared surprisingly attainable.

Clearly, I had to experiment.

I stepped outside, paced off a reasonable distance, timed myself—and I just edged it out.* Barely. And when I accounted for the added motivation provided by a T-Rex's breath on the back of my neck, I

---

*See page 7 for the formula, if you would like to see if you, too, could almost outrun a T-Rex.

gave myself a reasonable chance. That confidence only grew when I dug further. I studied the evasion strategies employed by prey animals and found they allowed these athletically outclassed animals to escape predators far faster than themselves. If I applied these techniques to my own life-and-death chase, the numbers suggested I would survive an encounter with the greatest hunter in the history of our planet.

The surprising discovery that I could use the latest research to conceivably survive an afternoon in the Late Cretaceous era with a starved tyrannosaurus nipping at my heels inspired further questions. With the benefit of hindsight and modern science, could a time traveler visit Pompeii and survive the eruption of Mount Vesuvius? Could they buy a third-class ticket on the *Titanic* and find their way off the sinking ship? Could they survive the Black Death? Could they escape the path of the most powerful tornado in history, ride alongside Magellan on his horrifically dangerous circumnavigation, or haul up stones to build Khufu's Great Pyramid?

In the process of discovering how a person could possibly survive these catastrophes and adventures, I found myself learning about these events in a far more granular way than a general history could ever provide. By focusing on hours, not eras, I felt the distance between the modern day and ancient history shrink to the proximity of a pursuing tyrannosaurus. Focusing on the individual's experience as the Gothic hordes poured into Rome or as an earthquake rocked San Francisco's peninsula during 1906, and then determining whether one should turn right or left, fight, hide, or flee, not only intensified and enlivened these bygone events, but delivered the kind of tangible information often neglected in vast-reaching histories.

The result is *How to Survive History*: a detailed, practical manual for surviving the greatest catastrophes and adventures in this planet's history. It's a how-to for finding food, shelter, and warmth in the face of history's most spectacular disasters. I've scoured every resource to come up with the likeliest way to survive each destination. I've read the diaries of the survivors, studied the accidents, and read the postmortems. I've looked at old maps or made my own when there weren't any, and I've published them here where applicable. I've asked the world's leading experts what they would do if they found themselves at the center of these great apocalypses, and report their answers, illuminating their disagreements and explaining their reasoning.

I've taken no speculative liberties save those necessary when history has obscured the precise details. There's no way to know, for example, the timing and path for every ejected lava bomb during the Pompeii eruption, and therefore it's possible the path I recommend would place you directly beneath a falling hunk of smoldering rock. I can only tell you the path where that is least likely to happen. In other words, survival is not guaranteed.

This guide is not a work of fiction or fantasy (save, of course, for the time-traveling reader's presence). It remains as faithful to actual events as the historical record allows. I have not fictionalized any of the events, nor have I conjured any dangers. I have not skirted any uncomfortable truths, nor conveniently ignored any threats.

I have, however, made a few assumptions. I have assumed that, like any good traveler, you're familiar with the local language, customs, and dress, where applicable. Xenophobia runs deep in human history. In many of these locations, eras, and cultures, assimilation isn't just useful or courteous. It's lifesaving.

I have also assumed you're up-to-date on your vaccinations. The whooping cough vaccine may seem like an annoying anachronism now, but in many times and places you're going to have a bad time if you neglect it.

Finally, to avoid redundancy, I have skipped over some dangers inherent to nearly all eras past. For example, don't drink the water, do assume your doctor has little idea what they're doing, and when meeting a stranger, remember that historical rates of interpersonal violence approach war-zone-like levels.

In short, this book should be read as an entirely serious attempt to guide a visitor through our planet's greatest catastrophes and adventures using the benefits of hindsight and modern science. It's written for the modern time-traveling reader who wants to witness the most dramatic, destructive, and dangerous events in history—and come back alive.

Good luck!

HOW TO SURVIVE

THE DINOSAUR AGE

Let's say you want to visit the era when the most powerful predators in history attacked the largest land animals the planet has ever seen. You want to see eighty-ton reptiles, carnivores with jaws comparable to a car shredder, and an animal the size of a giraffe take flight.

So you travel back 70 million years to the Mesozoic era—back to the Dinosaur Age. In the warmed climate, you'll feel the sticky heat of the Louisiana bayous as far north as Montana. You'll notice the changed geography: the absence of Rocky Mountains and the Sierra Nevada, the sea covering the midwestern United States, the island of India.

Grass will have only recently evolved. So you'll see a few blades, but no grasslands—only ferns, ficus, figs, cycads, and ginkgoes, along with large trees and dense forests. You'll also see the famous *Tyrannosaurus rex*.

Unfortunately, it will see you too.

You might think your only chance would be to hide, stand still, play dead, or climb. But surprisingly—shockingly—recent evidence suggests that you might be able to run from the most powerful predator to ever walk this planet.

At least, if you know how to use your biggest advantage: your size.

If a mouse fell down a 1,000-foot mine shaft, the renowned evolutionary biologist J. B. S. Haldane once proposed, the mouse would rise, shake the dust off, scurry away, and maybe even get right back up to do it again. If a rat fell from the same height, however, it would die. A horse would splash, Haldane writes, and a human would break.

Haldane does not provide a colorful verb in his 1926 essay *"On Being the Right Size"* for what would occur if a nine-ton *Tyrannosaurus rex* fell into that mine. But the giant predator would scream down the shaft at 172 miles per hour, hit the ground with 120 tons of force, and . . . shatter? Dismember? Detonate? Erupt?

Regardless of the proper descriptor for the *T. rex*'s disturbing demise, the purpose of Haldane's gruesome thought experiment was to demonstrate the dramatically different relationships that large and small animals have with gravity. This relationship, and the differing fates of the mouse and the rat, are explained by the "square-cube law," which states the simple fact that, as an object expands, its volume cubes while its surface area merely squares.

Because a falling animal's surface area increases its air resistance while its mass determines the force of its impact, the falls of various animals can be thrilling, tragic, or messy, depending on small differences in size. This may be a simple concept, but because a cubed number grows so much faster than a squared one, it is exceedingly difficult to intuit what the effects of small differences in size will be. That's particularly true with regard to the largest land animals to have ever walked the earth, especially if you have to outrun them.

When the T-Rex takes an interest in you, you may see its long legs and powerful muscles and think you should hide. Don't. You have the disproportionate effects of size on your side. The T-Rex's eruptive demise at the bottom of the mine shaft illustrates the most important factor to consider when facing this giant saurian's pursuit. In the run for your life, its awe-inspiring, terrifying, stupefying size would be, in fact, your greatest advantage.

A full-grown *Tyrannosaurus rex* was absurdly huge and absurdly powerful. It had rows of teeth it could push through triceratops bone. It could toss human-sized chunks of meat sixteen feet into the air with its jaws. It was as tall as a giraffe and, at nine tons, as heavy as an elephant. "*Tyrannosaurus rex* had proportionally more muscles devoted to its movement than nearly any animal that's ever lived," says Eric Snively, a biologist at Oklahoma State University who studies the biomechanics of dinosaurs. And yet if you see one, you should be only mildly concerned, because a tyrannosaur couldn't run.

I asked John R. Hutchinson, lead author of a 2002 paper published in *Nature* titled "*Tyrannosaurus* Was Not a Fast Runner," what a tyrannosaurus's performance in a race would look like. "A short-distance jog is about the best we'd expect," he said. "And not with a fast start, either."

The incredibly powerful, long-legged tyrannosaurus was slow for the same mathematical reason its demise in the mine shaft would be so eruptive. Like surface area, bone strength only squares as volume cubes. The result is that, as an animal increases in size, it requires proportionally more muscle and leg bone to stand, move, and run. Beyond a certain size, running becomes physically impossible, which is why giants and King Kong only exist in fairy tales. For all its muscular bulk, the *Tyrannosaurus rex*'s leg bones would have shattered under anything more than the stress of a brisk walk. Judging by its mass, muscle, and bones, Snively doesn't believe an adult tyrannosaurus could have moved faster than 12 or 13 miles per hour. Though 12 miles per hour approaches the top speed of a typical human depending on their conditioning—it equates to a twenty-second 100-meter dash—the *T. rex*'s slow acceleration would give the average runner a good chance of outsprinting or outmaneuvering the lumbering predator.*

Of course, the *Tyrannosaurus rex* would hardly be your only concern in the Mesozoic era. Numerous other meat-eating dinosaurs of various sizes might take an interest in snacking on you. Once again, whether you could outrun them or not depends on their weight.

In 2017, biologist Myriam Hirt and colleagues, studying animal movement at the German Centre for Integrative Biodiversity Research, asked a simple question: Is there an optimum size for speed? And the surprisingly simple answer, they discovered, is yes. When Hirt plotted the weight and speed of every running, swimming, and flying animal on earth, she found that, regardless of mode of movement, size and speed follow a parabolic curve. Both the smallest *and* the largest animals are the slowest. She concluded that if you were designing an animal for speed, it should weigh approximately 200 pounds. A bit heavier for a swimmer, a bit lighter for a flyer.

Hirt's discovery not only suggests that you should fear the mid-sized dinosaurs most, but, perhaps even more important, that you don't need to fear the largest at all. Regardless of strength or design, it would be physically impossible for the largest dinosaurs to outrun a human in good physical condition. The reason, Hirt tells

*Admittedly, there is some concerning speculation that *T. rex* hunted in packs, which would complicate your escape. Thankfully, the best current evidence suggests that, though they may have killed in packs like crocodiles, they did not coordinate their pursuits like wolves.

me, is a result of the interplay between power, acceleration, and the metabolism that fuels both.

An animal's top speed is the meeting point of two factors. The first is its total muscle power, which scales proportionally with its mass. The second is its ability to accelerate that mass, which does not scale proportionally. Acceleration relies on anaerobic muscle, which uses a stored fuel called ATP to power its rapid contractions. These so-called fast-twitch muscles produce the rapid, powerful contractions needed for acceleration. But ATP capacity is finite, it quickly depletes, and its capacity is determined by metabolism.

For reasons that aren't totally understood, an animal's energy production—metabolism—decreases proportionally to its mass (more precisely, it decreases to the power of 0.75). This reduction makes larger animals more energy efficient than smaller ones. If humans had a metabolism proportional to that of a mouse, for example, we would have to eat around twenty-five pounds of food per day. Larger animals are thus more efficient, but the cost of this efficiency is proportionally less ATP energy to accelerate.

By creating a simple formula that represents the balance between strength and acceleration, Hirt predicted the speeds of animals based upon nothing but their weight.

Thanks to the limits of metabolism and mass, we can eliminate every dinosaur weighing more than 6,000 pounds as a predatory threat. There is likely no animal of that size or larger—neither today, nor at any point in history—that a young, well-conditioned human couldn't outrun.

Unfortunately, there are numerous predatory threats that weigh substantially less. Hirt's discovery reveals a speed limit on the largest dinosaurs, but beneath that limit an animal's size is not the only determinant for its speed. Clearly, two species of roughly the same weight—such as, say, the human and the cheetah—can run at dramatically different speeds depending on their body design.

So before you lace up your running shoes, you need to know the precise speed of your foe. You need to know if you're betting your life on a race against a reptilian roadrunner.

But how does one determine the precise speed of an extinct species based upon nothing but bones and a few fossilized footprints?

Fortunately, in 1976 British zoologist Robert McNeill Alexander made the remarkable observation that all animals—from ferrets to rhinos—run with a "dynamically similar" gait. "Dynamic similarity" is an engineering term used to refer to motions that can be made the same simply by changing their scale—like swinging pendulums of different sizes. Alexander's discovery enabled paleontologists to estimate a dinosaur's running speed based on nothing but its hip height and stride length for the same reason the swinging frequency of a pendulum can be predicted by knowing only its length and swing angle.

Unfortunately, it's no more than a rough formula with the possibility of serious error, Hutchinson tells me. For example, Alexander's formula suggests that the carnivorous three-ton *Albertosaurus* ran 22 miles per hour. That would give you some possibility of escape. But there is a chance it ran more like a cheetah. In which case . . . good luck.

In 2020, the paleontologist Alexander Dececchi combined Hirt's and Alexander's formulas, along with recent archaeological discoveries of dinosaur fossils, to estimate the speeds of seventy-one different dinosaurs. And though there are too many medium-sized, fast, and dangerous carnivores to make a complete compendium, we can look at a few species as examples. If the dinosaur you see has similar body dimensions to one shown below, expect a comparable athletic performance.

Note: Obviously, your level of concern should vary depending on your running speed. To determine mine, I used a simple formula* and found I can sprint around 15 miles per hour. I would suggest you do the same. But as a rough guide to human speed: A gold-medal contender in the 100-meter dash can run 27 miles per hour, a good high school sprinter might run 22, the average person like myself could hope to reach 15 given proper motivation, and a brisk jog is around 7.

Unless you're in contention for a gold medal or are, at the very least, a fast amateur sprinter, each of these dinosaurs will athletically outclass you. Still, all is not lost if one should attack. Studies of the chases between cheetahs and impalas and between lions and zebras prove that a prey animal like you has a few significant advantages.

Alan Wilson, a professor at the Royal Veterinary College at the University of London who studies locomotor biomechanics, attached accelerometers to these predators and their prey to calculate their exact speed, agility, and tactics—and came away with encouraging results. His measurements suggest the cheetah is capable of running at least 53 miles per hour, while its prey, the impala, tops out at a mere 40. Likewise, the lion can reach 46 miles per hour, while the zebra can run only 31. Despite their significant speed deficit, both the impala and the zebra successfully escape in two out of every three pursuits. And even though a lion runs slightly faster than an impala, it won't even attempt to chase one in an open field.

Wilson's findings suggest that a pursuing dinosaur should not be able to catch you unless it is significantly faster.

But that's if you know *how* to run. If you merely flee at top speed from these reptiles, the only way you'll exit the Mesozoic

---

*Use this formula to estimate your speed if you don't have an easier electronic method handy: Pace out 60 meters and 100 meters, then time how quickly you can run both distances. Divide 40 by the difference. So, 40 meters ÷ (your 100 meter time minus your 60 meter time) = your top speed in meters per second. 1 m/s = 2.2 mph.

DROMAEOSAURIDAE (AKA RAPTORS) / **MILDLY CONCERNING**

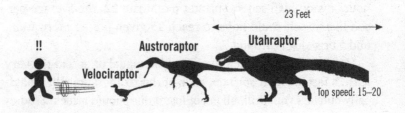

23 Feet

Austroraptor

Velociraptor

Utahraptor

Top speed: 15–20

ALBERTOSAURUS / **CONCERNING**

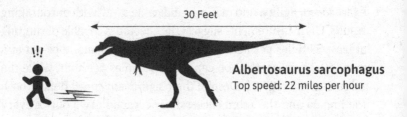

30 Feet

Albertosaurus sarcophagus
Top speed: 22 miles per hour

DELTADROMEUS / **VERY CONCERNING**

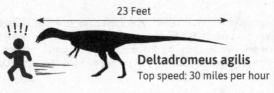

23 Feet

Deltadromeus agilis
Top speed: 30 miles per hour

Image to scale

era is as a coprolite.* Instead, to successfully escape a more athletic pursuer, you have to run smart. You have to use tactics. And above all, you must be unpredictable.

When Wilson's accelerometer measured the speeds of impalas fleeing from cheetahs, he discovered that even though they are capable of a blistering 40 miles per hour, in a race for their life they almost never ran faster than 31. The explanation for this surprising result, his study concludes, is that, at top speed, an animal sacrifices maneuverability. Their turning angles widen and thus their trajectory becomes predictable. Obviously, if a faster pursuer knows where you're going, you're dead.

When Wilson plugged in the athletic parameters of predator and prey into a computer model and ran simulations, he found two tactics that those being chased should employ. First, when the dinosaur begins chasing you but is still far away, change course frequently but do not decelerate. Second, when the predator draws within two or three strides, rapidly decelerate, turn sharply, and accelerate. Time this maneuver correctly and your pursuer's faster speed will result in a wider turn and a loss of a stride or two off the pace. When it catches up, do it again.

Your goal is to buy time. You have an endurance advantage. Recent studies like Dececchi's suggest some dinosaur species may have possessed remarkable endurance *for their size*—but your springy hips, stretchy Achilles tendons, and efficient cooling systems make you one of the greatest endurance runners nature has ever created. The longer the race, the greater your chances.

At some unfortunate point, however, the athletic disparity breaches a certain threshold, and no amount of correctly timed turns will be enough. That will likely be the case should you find yourself against what Snively tells me would be your most dangerous purser—the same *Tyrannosaurus rex* we've already dismissed,

*Fossilized dinosaur poop.

but with one significant difference. It's not the biggest, full-grown *T-Rexes* you should fear, says Snively.

It's the juveniles.

A FOURTEEN-YEAR-OLD *TYRANNOSAURUS REX* / TERRIFYING

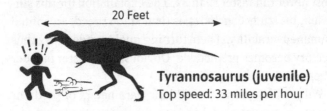

20 Feet

Tyrannosaurus (juvenile)
Top speed: 33 miles per hour

Unlike most animals, a tyrannosaurus is not its fastest as an adult. Instead, it reaches its peak speed in its youth, before it's slowed by its immense bulk. A teenage *Tyrannosaurus rex* runs an estimated 33 miles per hour, because it weighs a relatively lithe 2,000 pounds and yet already possesses jaws strong enough to tear through your bones. The young T-Rex is more likely to attack as well, because, unlike an adult, which hunts 7,000-pound duck-bill dinosaurs and five-ton triceratops, a teenage tyrannosaurus probably eats animals of your size.

If a young T-Rex attacks, then you'll have to resort to more devious tactics to survive (unless you're an Olympic sprinter—in which case you stand an impala-like chance of escape). You'll need the luck of a small cave to squeeze into or a thick bramble in which you can dive headlong. Or you can make your own luck by running the tyrannosaurus into a trap. Try laying a blanket of brush over a watering hole, a pit lined with stakes, or, if you prefer an eruptive result, over a very deep mine shaft.

HOW TO SURVIVE

THE CHICXULUB ASTEROID

Let's say you want to go on a camping trip with warm nights and sunny days, interesting wildlife and bright stars. So you travel back to the very, very Late Cretaceous period, for a camping trip 66.5 million years ago—back when the climate was so warm palm trees grew in the arctic and the most famous, most fearsome dinosaurs to ever live walked the earth.

You'll see the famous tyrannosaurus hunting the triceratops. You'll see the eighty-ton alamosaurus eating leaves forty feet above the ground. You'll see the tank-like ankylosaurus crushing opponents with its wrecking-ball tail. And just as you settle down on one particular evening, you'll see a brand-new star in the Northern Hemisphere sky.

The star won't flash, flare up, or blaze across the horizon. It will appear as stationary and as twinkly as all the others. But look again a few hours later and you might think this new star seems a little brighter. Look again the next night and it will be the brightest star in the sky. Then it will outshine the planets. Then the moon. Then the sun. Then it will streak through the atmosphere, strike the earth, and unleash 100 million times more energy than the largest thermonuclear device ever detonated.

The day the Chicxulub asteroid slammed into what is now the small town on Mexico's Yucatán Peninsula that bears its name is the most consequential moment in the history of life on our planet. In a prehistoric nanosecond, the reign of the dinosaurs ended and the rise of mammals began. Not only did the impact exterminate every dinosaur save for a few ground-nesting birds, it killed every land mammal larger than a raccoon. In a flash, Earth began one of the most apocalyptic periods in its history.

Could you survive it? Maybe.

If you make your camp on the right continent, in the right environment, and you seek out the right kind of shelter, at the right altitudes, at the right times, you might stand a chance, says Charles Bardeen, a climate scientist at the National Center for Atmospheric Research who modeled the asteroid's fallout for the *Proceedings of the National Academy of Sciences*. Of course, even if you are on the opposite side of the world at the time of impact—which is the only way you can hope to make it out alive—he recommends you act quickly. As soon as you hear the sonic boom (don't worry—you'll hear it regardless of where you are on the planet), get yourself to high ground and find underground shelter. Immediately.

You might think it's a bit alarmist to duck and cover from the impact of a city-sized rock landing 10,000 miles away. It isn't—but you wouldn't be the first to make the mistake of underestimating an asteroid. The cataclysmic risk posed by asteroids wasn't well understood until World War I. Before then, most astronomers operated under the blissful naivete that massive impacts like Chicxulub were simply not possible.

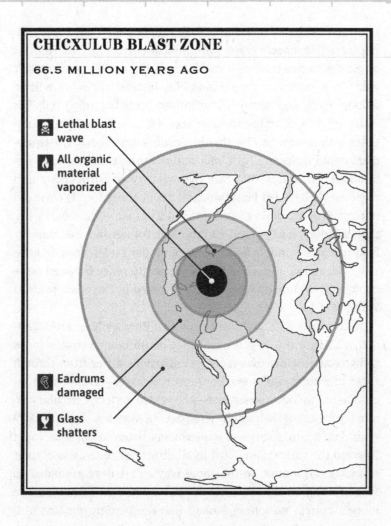

CHICXULUB BLAST ZONE

66.5 MILLION YEARS AGO

☠ Lethal blast wave

🔥 All organic material vaporized

👂 Eardrums damaged

🍷 Glass shatters

When Galileo trained his telescope on the moon in 1609 and discovered perfectly circular craters dominating its topography, astronomers began to wonder how they formed. A few, like the early nineteenth-century German astronomer Franz von Paula Gruithuisen, proposed asteroid impacts as the cause. But most rejected this theory based upon one simple, supremely confounding fact: The moon's craters are almost perfect circles. And, as anyone who has thrown a rock into dirt can tell you, that isn't what an impact scar should look like. Instead, the mark will be oblong, oval, and messy. (Gruithuisen probably didn't help his cause by also claiming to have seen cows grazing upon moon grass in these craters.) Further misleading any theorists, astronomers could make out little mountains in the center of each depression. Thus, for 300 years the majority of astronomers and physicists believed at least two facts about our moon: 1) cows did not graze upon moon meadows; and 2) lunar volcanoes, rather than meteors, had pocked its face. The former fact has thus far held true even under the scrutiny of modern telescopes, but the latter began to falter when a significant difference between large explosions and thrown rocks was revealed in the years prior to World War I.

In the early 1900s, astronomers like Russia's Nikolai Alexandrovich Morozov* began observing bomb craters and made a rather startling discovery: Large explosions differ from thrown rocks in a number of ways, but most relevantly—at least with regard to our moon's appearance—they leave perfectly circular craters regardless of their angle of impact. As Morozov wrote in 1909 after conducting a series of experiments, asteroid impacts would "discard the surrounding dust in all directions regardless of their translational motion in the same way as artillery grenades do when falling on the loose earth." After Morozov's findings, the moon's craters no longer looked like the benign remains of a

---

*Morozov's biography reads a little like *The Count of Monte Cristo* if you replace revenge with science. He spent twenty-five years as a political prisoner in a fourteenth-century castle turned prison on a small island outside Saint Petersburg, during which time he taught himself eleven languages and published works on everything from the structure of the atom to the geology of the Western Caucasus. Shortly after his release, he turned his attention to astronomy.

remote geologic process, but the circular harbingers of the apocalypse.

Even before Morozov's discovery, proponents of the volcanic moon theory, such as Harvard dean of science Nathaniel Shaler, were aware that an asteroid impact could be devastating. "The fall of a bolide of even ten miles in diameter . . . would have been sufficient to destroy organic life of the earth," wrote Shaler in 1903. But most astronomers believed this was an entirely theoretical exercise, partly because, as Shaler noted in his defense of the lunar volcanism theory, the very existence of humanity proved this sort of impact could not have occurred.

Morozov's calculations changed that. Once you know the true origins of the scars on the moon, you don't have to be an astronomer—or even own a telescope—to arrive at the sobering conclusion that asteroid impacts occur with disturbing frequency. Shaler was, in a way, presciently incorrect. An asteroid of nearly the size he described *did* impact Earth and *did* wipe out the planet's dominant species. Only, rather than wiping out humans, it cleared the evolutionary path for a shrew-sized placental mammal to eventually crawl, walk, and consider this camping trip to the apocalypse.

The survival of your shrew-like ancestor suggests that a fellow mammal like yourself would at least stand a chance. Unfortunately, the shrew had a number of apocalypse-friendly adaptations that humans have since lost. The shrew ate insects, burrowed away from the heat, and had fur to warm itself during the freezing decade that followed. You could replicate some of the shrew's survival strategies: You could burrow and you could expand your diet. But evolution has robbed you of others, and your opposable thumbs might not be enough to save you when that twinkling star enters the atmosphere at around 12.5 miles per second.

At impacts of that speed, Earth's atmosphere behaves like water. Smaller rocks—called meteors—hit the atmosphere like pebbles into a pond; they decelerate rapidly at high altitudes, either burning away in their friction with the air or decelerating to their low-altitude terminal velocity. But the mountain-sized Chicxulub asteroid hit our atmosphere like a boulder into a puddle. It maintained its velocity until impact, plunging through the entire sixty miles of atmosphere in around six seconds. As the asteroid screeched over what is now Central America, it emitted a sonic boom that reverberated across the continents.

It fell so quickly that the air itself could not escape. Under intense compression, the air heated thousands of degrees almost instantly, so that before the asteroid even impacted, much of the shallow sea that covered the Yucatán in the Late Cretaceous had already vaporized. Milliseconds later, the rock plunged through what water was left and slammed into bedrock at more than 10 miles per second. In that instant, a few near-simultaneous processes occurred.

First, the impacting meteor applied so much pressure to the soil and rock that these neither shattered nor crumbled but instead flowed like fluids. This effect actually makes it easier to visualize the formation of the crater, because the undulations of the earth almost exactly replicated the double splash of a cannonballer in a backyard swimming pool. The initial splash in all directions was followed by a delayed vertical *sploosh* when the cavity created by the impactor rebounded to the surface.

In a swimming pool, this entire process occurs in a few seconds. In Chicxulub, it took around ten minutes, but the difference is a function of scale, not speed. The initial wall of earth gouged outward was more than twenty miles high; the transitory cavity nearly breached Earth's mantle, and when the cavity rebounded to form the delayed "vertical sploosh," the earth rose at over 1,000 miles per hour to heights taller than Mount Everest. Within minutes this mountain almost entirely collapsed in a series of secondary explosions, but it left behind a smaller mound—called a crater's "peak ring," which is the formation that so confused those early moon gazers.

The very same moment the asteroid first struck the Yucatán and applied its pressure to the bedrock, it also converted the kinetic energy of a 7.5-billion-ton rock traveling 10 miles per second into heat. In an instant.

Why a rock hitting another rock produces heat isn't all that intuitive, but, thermodynamically, heat is simply the movement of molecules. The jigglier the molecules, the hotter the temperature. You can jiggle molecules by any number of means, but physically hitting them works, which is why a hammer heats up after you hit a nail. But whereas a hammer swing delivers approximately 0.0001 kilojoules of energy, the Chicxulub impactor delivered approximately 1,300,000,000,000,000,000,000,000. The impact jiggled the molecules of the earth's rock, soil, and air to temperatures that exceeded the surface of the sun.

The heat ripped away electrons from atoms, ionizing the air into an expanding fireball of plasma turbocharged with vaporized rock and blasted out from the impact crater at hypersonic speeds. The heated, rapidly expanding air and near-instantaneous conversion of earth to gas combined with the impact shock wave of the meteor itself to form a massive blast wave of pressure expanding outward at more than 1,000 miles per hour.

"The only comparable event is a shallow-depth thermonuclear explosion. Though, depending on their sizes, the energy associated with meteoric impacts can be much greater," says planetary scientist Elizabeth Silber. In this case, the impact was 100 million times greater. If this asteroid hit in the same spot today, the blast wave would kill you in Texas, deafen you in New York, and blow out your windowpanes in Buenos Aires.

The rock rang Earth like a bell. Waves in the earth's crust

radiated away from the impact zone at 2.5 miles per second. These waves then triggered fault-slipping earthquakes across the continents.

If you're on the other side of the world, you can expect to feel the ground-shaking effects thirty minutes after impact. Stay away from the banks of any large body of water, where earthquakes may trigger tsunami-like seiche waves in isolated bodies of water, like fjords or lakes. Even more important, stay off the beach.

The impact triggered tsunamis—*plural*—as tall as skyscrapers. The first of them hit gulf coastlines within the hour. Waves ranging from 600 to 1,000 feet high smashed into what is now Mexico and the southern United States and flooded tens of miles inland. The waves temporarily reversed the flow of rivers, rushing up riverbeds like thirty-foot tidal bores.

Tsunamis wrapped up the eastern seaboard, smashed into the eastern coast of the United States, and, six hours after impact, crested as 600-foot-high walls of water in Europe, Africa, and on the Mediterranean coasts. Within fifteen hours of impact, waves arrived on every coastline on the planet.

These tsunamis deeply complicate your survival strategy, because proximity to the coastline is otherwise a good idea in super-large asteroid strikes. The ocean serves as the earth's great insulator, moderating the severe temperature swings that the massive impacts induce. In the case of Chicxulub, the swing began with heat.

When the asteroid punched a hole into Earth's crust, it launched 25 trillion tons of the Yucatán Peninsula on ballistic trajectories. Some of this debris rocketed away at speeds that exceeded our planet's escape velocity, exiting Earth's gravitational pull to either orbit the sun or embed themselves in other moons or planets as meteors themselves. Thousands of these rocks from the ejected Yucatán eventually pelted Mars and a few even impacted Jupiter's moons, but the majority of the debris returned back to Earth within the hour. These glass-like chunks, called tektites—some as large as school buses, but most the size of marbles—pelted the earth at speeds ranging from 100 to 200 miles per hour.

Regardless of where you are on Earth, you'll need to find protection from this fiery hailstorm. Charles Bardeen suggests a cave.

As these glass bullets fell, their friction with the atmosphere collectively emitted enough thermal radiation to set fires across the world. By some estimates, the combined heat of the returning embers was the equivalent of a home oven set to broil. Most of the world's trees burned, which is perhaps why only ground-nesting bird species survived the impact. Of the few larger land animals to avoid extinction, nearly all had some means of escaping the heat. They either could burrow—like small mammals, snakes, and lizards—or escape into water, like crocodiles or turtles.

This suggests that, even if you're on the other side of the world, you'll need to find protection from the initial heat blast.

Bardeen suggests a *deep* cave.

In a final piece of terrible luck for the dinosaurs (and you), Chicxulub happened to strike an area rich in oil and sulfur. The impact ejected 100 billion tons of vaporized sulfur and 10,000 Lake Superiors worth of water into the atmosphere, which then condensed into massive storm clouds and fell back as torrents of acid rain. In the higher latitudes, continent-wide snowstorms deposited tens of feet per day. But the global inundation didn't last long because, in addition to water, Chicxulub vaporized and forcefully ejected enough oil to fill 150 football stadiums. This oil then condensed in the stratosphere as a black sooty layer, which covered the earth like a coat of black paint.

Unlike the sulfur and wildfire smoke, this carbon layer circulated high above the clouds, preventing rain from wicking it clean. So while rain cleared the immense plumes of wildfire smoke from the atmosphere after a few weeks, the soot layer persisted, reducing the amount of sunlight that reached the earth's surface by 90 percent for at least three years and dropping the planet into a deep, prolonged freeze. Global temperatures fell by an average of almost 50 degrees.

The only places you can go to avoid this global freeze are the tropical islands of Madagascar, India (at the time an island), and Indonesia. Not only do these equatorial oases provide a few plants and animals to eat, but according to climate models they are some of the few places on earth that continued to receive fresh

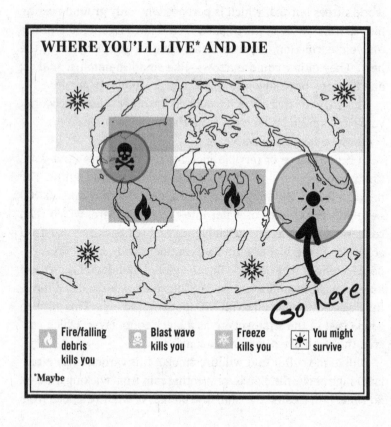

WHERE YOU'LL LIVE* AND DIE

Fire/falling debris kills you

Blast wave kills you

Freeze kills you

You might survive

Go here

*Maybe

water. In the global chill, evaporation almost ceased and rainfall decreased by 80 percent. Nearly every spot on earth outside of these tropical islands dried into a desert.

These islands might be an apocalyptic oasis, but they are no paradise. Skip the sunscreen and pack extra food. They receive 10 percent of their normal sunlight and only barely enough rainfall to stay above desertification. In this cold, dim environment, most—but not all—food chains will collapse.

Fossil evidence suggests freshwater ecosystems fared among the best, so forage near rivers or estuaries. There, you may find turtles, crocodiles, and some fish to eat. Sediment-living animals, such as clams, snails, and small crustaceans, also do quite well in the postimpact environment. Still, Bardeen warns against any trips by the ill-prepared. "To survive, you would have to bring something to keep you warm, and at least six years of food supply to stand any chance," he says.

But if you cannot be dissuaded, then at least find a mountainous tropical island. There you'll find a tolerable temperature and at least a little rain. You'll find shelter from the rain of tektites, the searing heat, and perhaps something to eat in the rivers and lakes. Just spare any shrew-like creatures you may find in your desperate search for food. It's unclear how many survived the Chicxulub impact, so eating the wrong one could result in some rather catastrophic consequences for the rest of humanity.

HOW TO SURVIVE

THE ICE AGE

Let's say you want to visit the era when glaciers taller than skyscrapers covered Canada, Scandinavia, and northern Europe. You want to live side by side with humans, hyenas, bears, wolves, reindeer, woolly rhinoceroses, mammoths, and lions. You want to see if you can survive in one of the coldest places on earth during one of the coldest periods in human history. So you travel back 25,000 years to see springtime in the vast, frigid mammoth steppe of what is now eastern Europe.

You'll see the mighty glaciers. You'll shiver beneath the mile-high walls of ice. You'll cower in front of the prowling leopards and stalking cheetahs. And then, a few hours after your arrival, you'll feel the first pangs of hunger. Unfortunately, here on these high, dry plains, archaeological evidence suggests an extraordinarily limited menu. In the refuse pile of one human camp, mammoths comprise 98 percent of all bones found. The bad news, then, is that if you want to eat here on the steppe, you'll have to pursue the most dangerous prey humans have ever hunted: the great woolly mammoth.

Mammoths were so dangerous that it wasn't until recently that archaeologists became convinced humans ever pursued them. Many scholars suspected that Stone Age hunters scavenged the mammoths found in their camps, rather than hunted them. But the mammoths' ages at the times of their deaths suggest hunter selection rather than natural demise. And paleoarchaeologist Piotr Wojtal removed any doubt when he found a smoking gun: a 24,000-year-old flint arrowhead still lodged deep in a mammoth's rib.

The evidence is by now unequivocal: Stone Age steppe cultures not only hunted mammoths, they did so to near exclusion. In modern times, the great woolly mammoth's close and similarly sized relative, the six-ton African elephant, occasionally kills poachers armed with guns. You'll have stick and stone. Nevertheless, as you grow hungry on the cold steppe, you may have only one option: launch a small stick with a sharpened rock point at a minibus-sized animal armed with twin eight-foot-long ivory spears.

And yet even before you earn the privilege of placing yourself near the business end of the pissed-off six-ton creature, you'll have to survive in a climate that is far different, and in many ways far more punishing, than anything you could possibly experience in the modern world.

Colloquially, the era in which you find yourself is referred to as the Ice Age, but that's a confusing misnomer, says Nicholas Swanson-Hysell, a professor of earth and planetary science at UC Berkeley, because we are still living through the very same "ice age." It began almost 3 million years ago when carbon dioxide levels in the atmosphere first began to plummet.

Carbon dioxide in the atmosphere serves as our planet's insulation. It traps heat otherwise headed for deep space, so its quantity dictates the earth's temperature. In eras when it has been elevated—such as in the Triassic, when its atmospheric concentration soared to 2,000 parts per million—you could have bathed above the Arctic Circle on a fern-forested beach. And when carbon has dropped—such as in the Cryogenian, when it plunged below 40 parts per million—ice has encrusted the equator.*

Because rocks contain the vast, *vast* majority of the earth's carbon, prior to the industrial revolution only volcanism spewed the significant planet-warming amounts of carbon dioxide into the atmosphere. At the end of the Triassic, for example, a 500-year eruption released a million cubic miles of lava and vented as much carbon dioxide into the atmosphere as all human activity in the twenty-first century. The planet warmed by 5 degrees, and three quarters of the world's species died.

But just as carbon enters the atmosphere with the destruction of rocks, it also exits with their creation. When carbon dioxide dissolves into water and encounters calcium and magnesium from freshly eroded mafic rock, the minerals and carbon react (in a process called "weathering") and settle on the ocean floor as vast beds of limestone.

In other words, the life cycle of carbon looks something like this:

      Rocks——VOLCANO!——air——ocean——rocks.

Volcanic eruptions might be more dramatic than the rather mundane chemical reaction that creates limestone, but the process has an equally profound, if diametrically opposed, environmental effect. When inordinate quantities of fresh mafic rock erode into

---

*Prior to the industrial revolution, the atmosphere contained 278 parts per million of carbon dioxide. Today, it is up to 417 parts per million, which is a level that throughout history has corresponded with no permanent northern ice sheets. That there still are ice sheets is simply because carbon levels have risen incredibly quickly and the temperature is still catching up. Right now, Earth is like a bag of frozen peas sitting in a freezer after the plug has just been pulled. The planet will thaw, but it will take some time.

water, the rock's minerals react with the atmosphere's carbon to create huge limestone beds. Earth loses its insulation, and the planet enters an ice age.

Of course, an increase in erosion sufficient to lock up enough carbon to send the planet into a prolonged freeze doesn't occur with the occasional mudslide. It occurs with the creation and erosion of entirely new islands and new mountain ranges. It occurs when continents and volcanic arcs collide and uplift huge amounts of fresh rock loaded with calcium and magnesium—and even then, only when those mountain ranges arise in the warmest, wettest, most erosion-friendly places. In other words, ice ages have an inciting incident—and it is always the same: a tectonic collision in the tropics.

Three million years ago, the Indonesian archipelago slammed into northern Australia. Millions of tons of fresh mafic rock uplifted into torrents of warm rain, calcium and magnesium flowed into the ocean, locked away gigatons of carbon into beds of limestone, and the earth's temperature plunged.*

Yet even within ice ages, the earth warms and cools as a result of cyclical changes in its orbit. Like a spinning top, the planet wobbles ever so slightly as it spins. These wobbles occur on 40,000-year cycles, and as Earth increases its tilt its hemispheres receive less winter sun, altering the ocean's currents in ways that cause the sea to sequester more carbon. The Northern Hemisphere reached the nadir of its wobble 25,000 years ago, causing atmospheric carbon dioxide to plummet to 65 percent of preindustrial

*The beautiful balance in this cycle, which keeps Earth's climate from swerving too far beyond an equilibrium, is that the chemical weathering process that sequesters carbon in rocks happens more efficiently in heat. So the warmer the planet becomes, the more carbon is removed—and vice versa. For this reason, Swanson-Hysell tells me, the earth will eventually remove the excess carbon we're emitting into the atmosphere. The bad news is that this process takes a few hundred thousand years. So the planet will, eventually, be fine. The fate of humanity is far less clear.

levels and the average global temperature plunged 15 degrees below what it is today. With the earth's insulation ripped away, massive ice sheets covered much of its Northern Hemisphere.

As you look around this new world of ice you have arrived in and try to understand the environment, your tendency might be to take what you already know about the current European steppe and drop the temperature 15 degrees. That simple formula would suggest you've found yourself in an arctic tundra like those of modern northern Canada or Russia. But both examples are wrong, as is your attempt to liken your current environment to anything you would find on earth today.

This is a tricky cognitive pitfall to avoid: Unlike in the Dinosaur Age, many animals will be familiar to you, but they'll appear in what seems like a bizarre biological juxtaposition. You'll see what you thought were animals that lived only in the African savannah grazing next to arctic ones. You'll observe arctic fox, bison, and reindeer—and all will seem normal. But then you'll watch a cheetah chase them. A rhino may graze next to a wolverine. A wolf may sit beside a lion. The result is an unsettlingly familiar landscape that falls into a kind of biological uncanny valley. If you spot a pack of lions racing after a reindeer—do not be alarmed. Well, maybe you should be alarmed. But at least you're not imagining things.

Instead of comparing where you are to what you know, start with this: You're in a cold, arid environment filled with sunny days and very little clouds or rain. Yearly rainfall approaches desert levels thanks to the Scandinavian ice sheets deflecting moisture from the Atlantic. Yet these same glaciers produce soil with fantastically productive potential thanks to constant replenishing from glacial deposits. The result is an incredible faunal dichotomy between the watered river valleys and the desert-dry highlands in the mammoth steppe. The elevated plateaus and mountain terraces resemble polar deserts, while the watered soil of the river valleys explode in productivity. The floodplains of the mammoth steppe's rich soils create an ideal grazing environment for the large, nomadic herd animals such as bison, horses, woolly mammoths—as well as the big-game hunters capable of bringing them down. These include wolves, lions, cheetahs—and, of course, humans. The people you see here are members of what archaeologists now call the Pavlovian culture. You'll find their camps located above river valleys where people can look out over vast grasslands, observe the mammoth herds that graze on them, and plan their hunts.

Mammoth hunting is not a solo pursuit, which means that, as you hunger, you'll need to make friends. But that may not be as hard as you might think. In popular culture the Pavlovians are often depicted with large clubs, tiger skins, and a general oafishness. But among archaeologists they're renowned for their sophisticated clothing, artwork, and intricate ivory bone carvings of voluptuous female figures—known as Venus figurines.

Fortunately for you, the expert view provides a far more accurate portrayal than the popular one.

Cognitively, the Pavlovians are an entirely modern group of *Homo sapiens* who are at least as smart as you—and certainly smarter in regard to everything that matters here. They have wildly different religious beliefs and different customs than you, but they do have religious beliefs and they do have customs. Like all other people, they argue, joke, gossip, laugh, love, fight, make jewelry, paint beautifully, smile when they're happy, scowl when they're upset, sing, play music and probably dance to it. They pray, tease, fight, play, coordinate sophisticated hunts, and surely have societal rules and norms as varied and complex as those of modern cultures.

They're also remarkably tall. And not just for their era, but for *any* era. The men average just over six feet in height—equal to the average height in the tallest country in the world today. They have brown eyes and dark skin that they protect from the average winter temperatures of negative 4 degrees Fahrenheit with sophisticated, parka-like clothing composed of furs from local arctic foxes, wolves, and wolverines, which they catch using fiber nets and traps.

Because there are few trees or wood here of any kind, they burn bones for their fires. If you want to survive this cold and metabolically expensive lifestyle, then you, like them, need a meal high in protein and fats. Where you are, that means mammoths. When you get hungry, it's that or starve.

To hunt mammoths, you need to first craft a spear with a shaft made of wood or bone and a spearhead of chipped flint. You might think you should throw this spear. Don't. Your target is a six-ton animal with an inch-thick hide. The spear will merely anger it, and you will die. Instead, you need to build a spearthrower.

A spear-thrower—also called an atlatl—is a short, flat stick with a spear-holding hook on one end and a handle on the other. Its simple design belies a deadly effect: By adding another lever to your throwing motion, the spear-thrower turns your mammoth-tickler into a formidable weapon. An experienced thrower can use an atlatl to launch a spear at over 100 miles per hour. The atlatl-launched flint spearhead Wojtal found in the mammoth rib traveled through four inches of the animal's skin and fat and then penetrated deep into its bone.

After crafting your spear and atlatl, you need to choose your camp. A hillside above a river valley where you can observe approaching mammoth herds is a necessity, but ideally this river valley should also lead into a natural trap.

The Pavlovian site in southern Poland where Wojtal discovered the flint spear buried in the mammoth rib is on a rocky promontory overlooking a natural cul-de-sac. "The area was a kind of trap," he explains, "isolated from three sides. From the north by a rocky cliff, and from the east and west by depressions and gorges."

You need to find a site like this. A place where you can drive a single mammoth into a dead end, so you have a chance to face it.

Choosing your target is also critical. Skeletal remains suggest even the mammoth-hunting specialists rarely attacked old bulls—even though these bulls likely traveled alone. The reason for this is obvious. Old males are large and highly aggressive, particularly if they're in musth—a period of heightened aggression in bull elephants when they're liable to attack everything from birds and giraffes to even trees. Rather than being shooed into a trap, a bull in musth may simply charge.

When I asked Wojtal how he would recommend taking down a mammoth, he suggested the approach of the people at the Kraków Spadzista site he studied: Isolate a mammoth from a group—perhaps one that seems weak or wounded—and herd it into the cul-de-sac. Once there, the game is simple.

"It was man against mammoth," says Wojtal. There's no evidence the Pavlovians at Kraków Spadzista ran mammoths over cliffs, or used ropes or underground pits or dogs—in fact, there's a great deal of evidence they did not. Rather, Wojtal tells me, the fight was as basic as it was brutal. "A furious animal with weight from one to six tons on one side, and a hunter with a stick on the opposite," he explains.

From the angle of the flint entry wound on the mammoth skeleton he found, Wojtal believes hunters faced the mammoth head-on and launched their spears in quick succession. It may seem dangerous to fire at the business end of a six-ton creature—and it is—but unfortunately you don't have a choice. Mammoth rears—like elephants'—were virtually impenetrable. There's no use, and in fact it would be extremely ill-advised to fire at a mammoth when its back is turned. It's the mammoth-hunting equivalent of blindsiding a bully with a spitball. You need to do more damage. You need to face the mammoth, and if you want the spear to carry enough velocity on impact, you need to be uncomfortably close. In other words, the best plan is to launch a weapon that by itself stands very little chance of disabling the animal, and a very high chance of angering it, from a very close range.

Wojtal tells me it's unknown how frequently the Pavlovian hunters died hunting mammoths—archaeologists haven't found nearly enough Pavlovian skeletons to draw any general conclusions. But he assures me your hunt won't be safe. If the spear hits, a full-grown six-ton mammoth may charge you at 20 miles per hour with lethal intent. Should you run, fight, or play dead?

According to the nineteenth-century Scottish big-game hunter Walter Bell's 1923 memoir *The Wanderings of an Elephant Hunter*,

WHERE TO SPEAR A MAMMOTH

25,000 YEARS AGO

Yes!

No!

6 feet

no advice in this scenario is useful. "An elephant's charge is a nerve-test of the highest order," he writes. Bell, who began his career at age sixteen hunting man-eating lions for the Ugandan railway, writes that an elephant's charge is so terrifying that any instructions he conveys to his readers are probably useless as "you won't have time to think of anything anyway." However, if you don't panic when the great mammoth charges, he suggests you stand your ground, continue to fire, and hope the charge is a false one.

You can take Bell's advice. You can stand and throw. But Bell had a gun. You have stick and stone. I have never hunted man-eating lions, but I think you should run.

Of course, don't run in a straight line. The mammoth is faster than you and thus will catch you in seconds. Instead, run below your top speed in the same zigzag pattern that saved you from the *Tyrannosaurus rex* (see chapter 1). The mammoth is about as large as a tyrannosaurus, but not nearly as mobile, so turn frequently and find something to hind behind—though keep in mind the mammoth can easily topple trees or move car-sized boulders.

If the mammoth runs you down, it will probably attempt to gore you with its tusks. Failing that, it will finish the job by stomping you. And here, where you are, an injury of any severity will be a fatal one.

But you can avoid this fate. Possibly. Just attack in a group. Avoid large mammoth herds and single aggressive males. Launch your spears in quick succession while facing the mammoth, hope it charges someone else in your group, and if you happen to be the unlucky one—run.

HOW TO SURVIVE

ANCIENT EGYPT

Let's say you want to spend a summer working outside, building a little muscle while getting a little dirty, a little exercise, and maybe a tan. So you travel back to Ancient Egypt's Old Kingdom for a summer job in the year 2550 BCE to work on the greatest community service project in human history: the tomb for the pharaoh Khufu. The Ancient Egyptians called it the Horizon of Khufu.

You probably know it as the Great Pyramid of Giza.

You'll work dawn to dusk for four months dragging stones weighing between one and eighty tons through the heat of an Egyptian summer with only one day off every thirty. You'll sleep in the open air, trudge behind multiton stones held in place by palm leaf ropes, wedge massive boulders into a face so steep and treacherous that at least 1,600 pyramid-climbing tourists fell to their deaths before the practice was banned. You'll endure a tour of physical labor so extreme a graveyard of pyramid workers suggests most suffered extreme arthritis, some lost limbs, and the average worker died at thirty-five years old. And you'll do it all wearing open-toed shoes.

But let's say you don't show up at just any time during the twenty-five-year construction. Let's say you join just as the pyramid reaches nearly half its eventual height. That would put you in Giza in time to help haul what might be the single most impressive and inexplicably placed rock in human history: an eighty-ton solid black granite slab as heavy as the largest moai stone somehow maneuvered onto the ceiling of Khufu's burial chamber 210 feet above the ground.

Watch your toes.

Most archaeologists believe the Egyptians built the entire 2-million-stone structure within twenty-five years, which means they must have, on average, quarried, hauled, and placed a 5,000-pound limestone block every five minutes during every daylight hour for an entire generation. Egyptologist and archaeologist Richard Redding tells me the project was so large it probably touched the lives of all 1 million Ancient Egyptians—implying a need for labor so extensive that, even if your résumé is light on pyramid-building experience, you shouldn't have much trouble landing the job.

As a stone-hauling pyramid builder, you will be among coworkers who are neither slaves nor full-time employees, but instead farmers, Redding explains, who Khufu conscripted for brutal four-month tours while they were idled by the Nile's annual summer flood. Contrary to popular myth, free Egyptians, rather than slave labor, built the pyramids. But that doesn't mean you'll be free to leave, either. Conscripted labor in Ancient Egypt doesn't have an exact modern equivalent, but it likely resembled the draft or obligatory military service. It was a tax Khufu applied on the local populace, but a tax of labor rather than of money. Not paying was not an option. The Ancient Egyptians punished tax cheats with beatings, imprisonment, and occasionally mutilation.

As a conscripted farmer, you'll sail down the Nile in mid-July, when the monsoonal rains that fell in the Ethiopian highlands reach Egypt and swelled the Nile far beyond its winter banks. The Nile's annual flood brought life to this otherwise desert country. Its sediment and water transformed the banks of this parched land into one of the most productive agricultural areas in the world. But the flood also idled the Ancient Egyptian farmers, who had to wait until the waters receded before they could return to their fields.

Join this workforce, and you'll ride the currents of the Nile from the farms in the south of Egypt and sail into a harbor dug into the Giza Plateau to allow the thousands of ships delivering the tools, stones, food, materials, and workers to flow directly to the enormous national project. When you arrive in the harbor, you'll see the massive half-built Pyramid of Giza rising 200 feet above the plateau, with its sides glistening in its white limestone cladding. But perhaps even more impressive than the pyramid itself is the massive work camp you'll see beneath it.

Egyptologists had long assumed the pyramid workers must have lived nearby, but they didn't discover the work camp until 1990, when a tourist riding on horseback tripped over a stone wall peeking above the sand and revealed a city of stunning sophistication and size.

Egypt's farmers in their daily lives had most likely never seen more than a hundred people at any one time, yet as they flowed into the Giza harbor they arrived in a work camp occupied by as many as 30,000. The camp wasn't just large for a work project; at its height, it was one of the world's largest cities. It contained bakeries, fish processing facilities, and stockyards all designed for mass food production. It had a series of large military-style barracks capable of housing at least 2,000 people—though, as a manual laborer, you won't merit a bed or even a roof. Initially, Redding tells me, archaeologists believed temporary manual laborers like yourself lived inside these cities. But now, he says, most believe the barracks would have been far too small to house the massive swell of seasonal workers. Instead, only boat crews and traveling VIPs likely slept in them. You're neither, so you'll sleep on the ground.

To fit in among the crew, you'll need to look the part. Egyptian men work in kilts with nothing underneath, while women wear long narrow dresses or sheaths with shoulder straps. Men often go shirtless—though you probably shouldn't. It regularly reaches 110 degrees, so add a linen shirt to protect your skin from the sun. Open-toed leather sandals are the typical footwear, even while wedging up multiton stones. Perhaps even more unfortunately, the traditional workman hairdo resembles a bowl cut.

Thankfully, the pharaoh feeds his workers well. Most farmers probably ate better while working at the pyramid than they did at home. The skilled, housed laborers ate a quarter pound of beef per day—a remarkable luxury considering cattle had to be herded from their distant pastures in the delta, and a single cow cost an Egyptian craftsman a year's worth of wages. Archaeologists have found so many bones they believe the camp consumed 4,000 pounds of beef daily, which would have required a herculean logistical effort to procure and stands as testament to the extraordinary resources Khufu put toward his tomb.

Unfortunately, while the skilled craftsmen merit this lavish expense, you do not. As a manual laborer, Redding says, you will probably eat catfish, goat, or cow's feet stew along with a chunk of stale bread, which you'll need to dip in your beer to soften. Beer seems like a perilous choice of beverage considering you'll soon be placing a multiton block on the edge of a very steep slope, but you need not be concerned. At least, not for your sobriety. Egyptian beer was more nutritious than alcoholic. It was a somewhat filling drink with the slight alcoholic tang of a kombucha.

After breakfast, with a belly full of beer, bread, and cow's feet, you'll set out with a twenty-man work team. If you are a member of the quarrying group, you'll receive a copper chisel. Copper is soft, and thus a poor metal for chiseling rock, but it's better than the era's alternatives. And because it was sourced from small copper mines across the Red Sea, it's expensive. So don't lose it. Egyptian authorities went to great lengths to ensure it was not lost or stolen, even going so far as to weigh the amount of copper each worker took into the field. If you return with less than you should, expect a consequential conversation.

Yet as a seasonal worker you won't quarry rock. Quarriers worked year-round preparing huge numbers of limestone blocks that would then be lifted into place when the swell of summer labor arrived. You are that labor. So, after breakfast, you and the rest of the crew will set out to haul rock.

You might think the mood would be somewhat morose among this conscripted crew whose taxes, time, and backbreaking labor was going toward a massive monolith in the middle of the desert. But hieroglyphic graffiti suggests an esprit de corps developed among these laborers. Work crews dubbed themselves team names like "The King's Drunkards" or "Friends of Khufu," competed against one another, and exchanged competitive banter. Rather than haul rocks in lonely misery, it seems they hauled rocks reveling in their collective misery.

Exactly how they moved those stones has been a matter of scholarly debate since the Ancient Greek historian Herodotus marveled at the pyramids in 450 BCE. Remarkably, despite images and writings that describe some of the minutest details of their lives, no hieroglyph yet found describes exactly how the Egyptians built their great pyramids. That ambiguity has caused everyone from the ancient Herodotus to Napoleon to speculate on their method—with theories ranging from pulleys to alien technology.

But Redding explains that recent archaeological discoveries provide a firm answer: There were no tricks—no aliens, nor barely any technology at all. Instead, he says, they used ropes, sleds, ramps—and the key ingredient: backbreaking, OSHA-disregarding, ligament-straining, and even limb-risking amounts of human pulling power.

Archaeologists have found evidence of the sledges and ropes, along with hieroglyphs showing how they used both. One image in the tomb of Djehutihotep shows 172 workers hauling a colossal fifty-eight-ton statue more than twenty miles over flat terrain using nothing but ropes, a sled, and a water-lubricated path. The Egyptians used this technique to pull the limestone blocks up ramps that they then disassembled after the pyramids' completion. But the design of that ramp system remains, as the Egyptologist Mark Lehner writes, "one of the thorniest problems in all of pyramid building."

The problem is that every design would have involved significant trade-offs. First, the ramp would have had to ascend at a reasonable grade to reduce strain on the lifting team. However, a long, gentle ramp to the top would have required more material than the entire pyramid itself. So that seems implausible.

Secondly, employing switchbacks—the typical solution to climb a steep grade—would require hauling teams to somehow navigate sharp turns while pulling stones with elongated ropes. Finally, using the pyramid face itself as a ramp would require unacceptably long ropes.

In other words, the pyramid builders must have constructed a ramp—but it could not have been a long one, it could not have been a short one, nor could it have taken any turns. You can see the problem. The theories various scholars have supported corresponds to whichever problem they see as slightly more surmountable than the others.

But Redding tells me recent archaeological discoveries in the Giza limestone quarry, which the pyramid builders dug just a quarter mile from the pyramid's base, have provided a firm answer to to Herodotus's ancient question. At the bottom of the quarry, beneath stone chippings and debris, archaeologists have found the remains of an old ramp that ascends to the surface at a reasonable 11 percent grade. Today, it stops at the top of the quarry. But if the ramp continued its trajectory, Redding explains, it would arrive at the pyramid's southwest corner at approximately 120 feet of altitude. That's only a quarter of the way to the top, but by then more than half of the limestone blocks would have been laid.

From there, Lehner proposes the ramp looped up and around the backside of the pyramid with gentle turns that haulers could navigate because the stones at the top of the pyramid trend smaller. Once the pyramid was complete, the builders disassembled the ramp and dumped its rocks into the obvious place—the giant pit they had just dug, which explains the massive piles of stone chippings found in the quarry.

It now seems clear that to move the blocks onto the pyramid the Egyptians weren't aided by advanced levers, alien technology—or really even any technology. They simply dragged them on sledges from the bottom of the quarry up a long, quarter-mile ascent at a grade twice as steep as the steepest highway in the United States.

Like any job involving hard manual labor, your first few days will be the most dangerous.

Before your body acclimatizes to Egypt's 100-degree summer heat, you won't sweat efficiently and your heart will beat too quickly. You're out of rock-hauling shape and unused to the kind of hydration required for working in these conditions. According

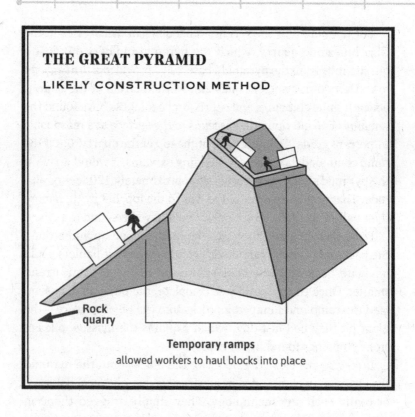

THE GREAT PYRAMID

LIKELY CONSTRUCTION METHOD

Rock
quarry

Temporary ramps
allowed workers to haul blocks into place

to OSHA, almost half of heat-related deaths occur on a worker's first day on the job, and more than 70 percent occur during the first week. If you experience dizziness, headaches, muscle cramps, or nausea, you need to retreat to the shade. If those symptoms progress to vomiting, faint pulse, or confusion—it may be too late. In modern times, an IV might save you. Here, there isn't even ice.

You may be tempted to cool off in the Nile, but you probably shouldn't. The river teems with the blood parasite schistosomes, a flatworm that burrows through the skin, travels through the venous system to the liver, matures, and lays eggs along the intestinal wall. Four to six weeks after infection, you'll develop a fever and become extremely lethargic. Eventually, the infection becomes chronic, and depending on where the eggs flow, they can cause intestinal disease, cancers, seizures, or death. Schistosomiasis is considered by the CDC to be the world's second most devastating parasite after malaria, and archaeologists have detected it on numerous Ancient Egyptian mummies.[*]

Workplace accidents will also be a significant problem.

Even climbing the pyramid will be dangerous—let alone while pulling, pushing, levering, and maneuvering multiton blocks on it. The pyramid's face wasn't vertical—but at 52 degrees it was close enough. If you fall, you'll slam down the sides before you finally hit the ground. Unsurprisingly, skeletons in the workers' cemetery in Giza show signs of significant fractures in their arms, legs, and hands. Fortunately, many of those fractures healed, suggesting doctors immobilized them in splints. Some even seem to have survived amputations. So if you're injured, it seems medical care is available—though whether you should accept it depends on your malady. Ancient Egyptian doctors were fairly proficient at caring for traumatic bone injuries. A papyrus describing treatment for a broken nose doesn't differ much from what you would receive today. But medications for internal or indirect causes of suffering such as arthritis, disease, or parasites were not nearly as effective. Medical papyri run legion with revolting prescriptions for diseases, including ointments of animal dung, and broths of dead flies and cooked mice. The list of prescriptions suggests that if the cause of your injury is obvious—say, if a falling rock crushes your arm—you should seek medical care. But if you sicken, you probably shouldn't.

As you drag each limestone block from the quarry to the work

---

[*]Having contracted this particular parasite, I can confirm that, if you become infected, you won't feel like hauling heavy rocks.

surface of the pyramid, you'll place it under the watchful eye of chief builder Hemiunu, one of Khufu's most powerful viziers and the director of all royal projects.* But far from inventing the architectural concepts necessary for the Great Pyramid's construction, Hemiunu owes a great architectural debt to Imhotep, and later to Khufu's father-king, Snefru. Imhotep was the healer, architect, and vizier to Khufu's great-grandfather King Djoser, and he invented the predecessor to the pyramid by innovating on the traditional Egyptian bench-like tomb known as a mastaba. Instead of building one bench to house Djoser's remains, he built a series of benches stacked on top of each other, like a giant wedding cake.

King Snefru took Imhotep's idea and improved upon it. He developed the building techniques necessary to turn Imhotep's wedding cake design into Egypt's famous smooth-faced pyramids, though that research hardly came without cost.

In his first two attempts at pyramid building, King Snefru made critical errors. He built his pyramids on soft ground and then compounded this mistake by angling the sides too steeply. The steep sides put tremendous pressure on the pyramid's outer edges, which gradually sank into the sand as the pyramid grew. Snefru's first try collapsed before completion, and his second, known as the Bent Pyramid, developed such severe cracks that he had to dramatically decrease the angle of the pyramid halfway through

---

*This has recently become a matter of some debate. For most of the twentieth century, Egyptologists believed Hemiunu to be the chief pyramid architect after deciphering hieroglyphs on his tomb beneath the Great Pyramid that identified him as such. But in 2013 archaeologists cast that claim into some doubt after discovering the diary of one of the pyramid builders at a site near the Red Sea. This remarkable papyrus—the oldest ever discovered—was written by an official named Merer who was charged with shipping the pyramid's white limestone blocks from their quarry in Tura to Giza. In it, Merer writes that Khufu's half brother Ankhhaf served as the project's director. You'll have to reconcile the debate.

construction, hence the name. Snefru did finish the Bent Pyramid, but due to aesthetic or stability concerns, he never used it. Instead, he learned from his failures and built Egypt's first successful true pyramid—the Red Pyramid—on a foundation of solid rock. He then passed on his knowledge, and his obsession, to his son Khufu and to his architect (and your boss) Hemiunu.

Hemiunu chose the Giza Plateau for his King Khufu pyramid likely because of its proximity to both the Nile and a suitable limestone quarry, as well as the quality of its strong limestone bedrock, which streaks from northeast to southwest through the plateau and explains the diagonal orientation of the three Giza pyramids.

Hemiunu clearly learned from Snefru's mistakes, as he not only chose to build on bedrock but paid meticulous attention to the pyramid's foundation. Modern architects calculate the Great Pyramid's base to be flat to within less than a half inch across an area almost ten football fields in size—a feat he accomplished using nothing but wood A-frames and plumb lines to carefully correct irregularities, yard by yard.

Hemiunu then oriented the faces of the pyramid in the exact cardinal directions with an error of less than .1 degree. He did this not by compass, but by carefully observing and then measuring the exact locations of the rise and fall of the night's stars. He then measured out the initial base of the pyramid using a stick called a cubit so that all four sides were perfectly equal. Finally, as the pyramid rose, he took continual measurements to keep the face at the proper angle and to keep the corners perfectly aligned.

His design required precision, expert masonry, and Snefru's hard-earned experience, but it didn't require remarkable mathematical ability or architectural genius. Khufu's Great Pyramid doesn't stand testament to Egypt's scientific or technological achievements, but it does testify to its remarkable bureaucratic ones. Constructing the pyramid represents an extraordinary marshaling of a nation's resources toward a single goal, like the Manhattan Project carried out over a generation. In order to build his great tomb, Khufu synchronized the movements of his entire nation toward a single purpose. He built one of the world's largest cities out of nothing; housed and fed its occupants for more than twenty years; arranged for the mining of copper from across the Red Sea; quarried and shipped black granite from Aswan and white limestone from Tura; and organized the conscription of tens of thousands of farmers every year. To build his Great Pyramid, Khufu reached into the lives of nearly every one of his more than 1 million subjects and bent them toward a single goal.

Khufu managed this massive organizational challenge by employing the most civil servants per capita in history, and then structuring his bureaucracy in a manner bearing remarkable resemblance to modern militaries. His tens of thousands of government employees of descending rank worked in four branches of government: the royal court, the army, the church, and civil government. To requisition the resources for his pyramid, employees of his treasury fanned out across the country and assigned each head of Egypt's forty-two regions (or "nomes") a tax. Because Ancient Egypt relied on a system of sophisticated barter rather than money, taxes were based upon whatever the region produced. The nomes of the Nile Delta, for example, paid in cattle, while in the south they paid in grain. Tax rates hovered around 10 percent, but rather than measure each farmer's production, which would have encouraged farmers to hide their crops, the treasury measured the height of the Nile's flood using "nilometers" and, referencing past years' production as a guide, assigned each region a tax based on how much they had historically produced under those conditions. During periods of pyramid construction, part of a region's tax included the four months of backbreaking labor you're now providing.

* * *

When I asked Egyptologist Colleen Darnell whether she had any advice for you as you labor, she told me Ancient Egyptian wisdom literature suggests the culture had clear mores: "Don't steal. Don't get drunk on the job. And people who complained were frowned upon," she says. So, as you rise to work on your twenty-eighth straight day hauling rocks in the heat beneath a summer Egyptian sun, try to keep a stiff upper lip.

Of all the dangers you face during your tour—a buffet of peril that includes parasites, heat, disease, food, and towering heights—nothing will compare to the life-threatening risk you confront the moment you line up to haul the eighty-ton black granite slab.

Judging by the Djehutihotep hieroglyph, Ancient Egyptians organized their pulling teams so that each puller pulled with approximately 150 pounds of force (roughly the same force required to pull a large car on a flat road). Studies of tug-of-war competitors suggest the average athlete can pull with 1.5 times their body weight. So while the weight is certainly possible if you're a healthy adult, it falls significantly outside the bounds of OSHA recommendations of 50 pounds. That fact probably explains the serious signs of degenerative back and knee arthritis found in the skeletons of thirtysomethings in the pyramid workers' cemetery. Fortunately, you can mitigate these degenerative injuries if you pull with proper technique.

To learn how to safely haul a rope, I turned to Mick Cooper, secretary for the English Tug of War Association, who tells me he has fifty years of tug-of-war experience. He offered a few pieces of advice: First, don't use a "heave-ho" strategy. "That's a technique employed by carnival teams competing for a barrel of beer," says Cooper. Serious competitors haul continuously. Second, keep your arms straight, lean back, and *push* with your legs. Amateurs often yell *pull* while hauling on a rope, but that's a mistake. Use your more powerful back and leg muscles to push, rather than pull, and lean back while doing so in order to keep your back straight. That should help avoid injury. In a study on the competitors in the 1998 Tug-of-War World Championships, back sprains composed almost half of the injuries. Hand injuries made up a significant portion as well. You can partially avoid those by never, ever wrapping the rope around your hands, fingers, or any other body part. Not only can tension in the rope easily crush body parts, but if your comrades fail, you could be dragged behind the sliding rock.

Unfortunately, there is an even more serious and gruesome tug-of-war danger when hauling such heavy weight. There are no diminishing returns when adding pullers to a rope, which is how hauling that eighty-ton granite block is even possible, but this also means the forces can scale far beyond what would seem intuitively possible. The Ancient Egyptians were clearly aware of this latent human pulling power, but the immense forces deployed by huge pulling teams have deceived more modern minds to occasionally tragic effect.

On June 6, 1995, a group of Boy Scouts in Frankfurt, Germany, lined up for a 650-person game of tug-of-war. When the two-inch-thick nylon rope broke, it snapped back with such speed it killed the two scouts standing in front and injured twenty-five others. Other large tug-of-war matches have severed arms, fingers, and crushed hands. On October 25, 1997, in Taiwan, 1,600 people applied 180,000 pounds of force to a rope rated for less than half that. The severed line ripped backward with such force it tore the arms off the two people in front.

If we assume the Egyptians used the same principles to pull the eighty-ton granite slab as the Djehutihotep hieroglyph depicts, then to haul the eighty-ton rock up the 11 percent grade you'll pull with at least 343 Ancient Egyptian pullers standing alongside.

Together, you'll be pulling with enough force to rip apart a half-inch piece of rebar. Fortunately, there's evidence that Egyptian palm-fibered ropes could withstand immense strain. Even so, when Hemiunu orders that eighty-ton stone block onto a sledge and directs you and 343 others to take your places along the ropes, you probably shouldn't stand in front.

HOW TO SURVIVE

POMPEII

Let's say you want to spend a warm summer day at a peaceful, seaside hub of Roman life. You want to walk fountain-lined streets, practice your Latin, play dice, snack on olives, and drink local wine made from grapes grown in fantastically rich volcanic soils. So you travel to the port town of Pompeii on August 24, 79 CE, and you arrive sometime between the hours of 9 and 10 a.m. That will give you enough time to explore and maybe even grab a loaf of bread for breakfast at the local bakery (see map on the next page for directions).

But it will also put you in Pompeii in time to experience a 5.9-magnitude earthquake, hear a distant boom echo through the streets, and see a black cloud rise from the nearby Mount Vesuvius. You'll watch as the towering volcano begins to disgorge 1.5 million tons of molten rock per second and release 100,000 times the thermal energy of the Hiroshima bomb.

All while you stand a mere six miles away.

Your situation seems challenging—but, surprisingly, it's not hopeless! When I emailed Pier Paolo Petrone, a forensic anthropologist at the University of Naples Federico II, asking if any

Pompeiians survived the eruption, he wrote back to say that many did. "But likely only those who took immediate action."

Unfortunately, instead of immediately evacuating, some Pompeiians took shelter from the falling ash. This may seem prudent, but it is a mistake.

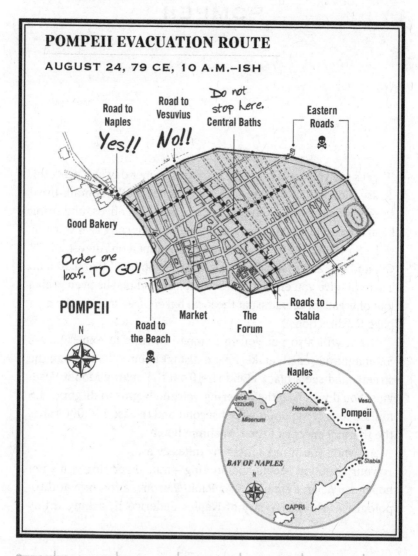

POMPEII EVACUATION ROUTE

AUGUST 24, 79 CE, 10 A.M.–ISH

*   *   *

Fortunately, you'll have time to leave, because the early stages of Vesuvius's eruption were not the most dangerous. The pressurized magma inside the magma chamber contained dissolved gas, and cracking Vesuvius's vent had the same effect as opening a gargantuan can of soda. The dissolved, superheated gasses rushed out of solution and blasted through the volcano's narrow vent at supersonic speeds. The effect was like a jet engine. As lava and searing gas blasted out of the mountain, the towering hell furnace sucked in the surrounding cool air, heated it, and created a rushing upward lift of superheated air that screamed toward the stratosphere.

This is good. The cloud was hot enough to melt lead, and the high atmosphere was the safest place for it. Eventually, these molten rock chunks cooled and fell, and because the wind on August 24 blew south-southwest, they dropped on Pompeii. At first, the initial pieces of lava fell like snow. But as the eruption continued, their density gradually increased until these pieces of pumice came down with enough size and ferocity to collapse houses.

But that took hours. You still have time.

Do not linger, however, because within Mount Vesuvius another, even more dangerous process began to take place. As the gasses within the magma chamber depleted, the eruption lost power. This may sound like a positive development. It is not.

When the mix of hot ash and gas in a volcanic cloud becomes too dense, its column will collapse. Instead of rising miles into the atmosphere, it will rise only a few hundred feet and then fall. As the cloud descends, it accelerates, so that when it reaches the ground it flows like a superheated sandstorm moving at autobahn speeds. These "pyroclastic flows" can be 1,800 degrees Fahrenheit, dense enough to suffocate you, and extend for miles. In the early morning hours of August 25, a pyroclastic flow killed everyone remaining in Pompeii. You need to leave long before then.

As to where to go, you have two choices. Mountains block your path to the east, and the Mediterranean Sea blocks your escape to the west. You could try to wait for a boat at the beach, but a) archaeologists have found a large group of bodies in a boathouse in nearby Herculaneum who appear to have attempted just that, b) the prevailing winds are against you, and c) earthquakes sloshing the Bay of Naples cause repeated tsunamis.

Your only two viable options, Petrone tells me, will be to run north, toward Naples, or south, toward the town of Stabiae. There are issues with both, but fortunately none of those issues involves melting in a river of lava.

This fear is natural in any volcanic eruption, but generally misplaced. Depending on its composition, lava ranges from 10,000 times to 100 million times the viscosity of water, which means even the runniest molten rock has the viscosity of room-temperature honey. Unless you're on a very steep slope, you can generally outrun it. These fiery rivers flatten stationary objects like houses, but "people can move out of the way," says Stephen Self, a volcanologist at UC Berkeley, ". . . usually."

Instead, it's the magma beneath the mountain, and its precise composition, that should deeply concern you. Different types of magma produce dramatically different eruptions. Watery magmas won't build up nearly as much pressure as thicker varieties and don't contain nearly as much gas, which means when they erupt they usually ooze rather than bang. A viscous magma, on the other hand, doesn't flow nearly as easily. These magmas require more pressure before they erupt, and therefore usually erupt less frequently. But when they do, they explode. Unfortunately for you, the magma inside Vesuvius is unusually viscous, which partly explains why its eruption registers as a formidable 5 out of 8 on the logarithmically scaled Volcanic Explosivity Index—the same as the Mount Saint Helens eruption in 1980. (Fortunately, VEI 8 eruptions are quite rare. The most recent one occurred on New

Zealand's Mount Taupo 26,500 years ago, and it destroyed an area the size of El Salvador.)

A volcano's explosive power largely depends on both how its magma forms and how it arrives at the surface, which, contrary to what one might assume, is not by bubbling up from the earth's molten core. Magma doesn't form when the sinking crust melts in the heat of the earth's depths, either—at least not usually—because pressure increases the melting point of rock by strengthening its chemical bonds. So even as the heat rises deep within the earth, so does the pressure, and the mantle remains solid.

Instead, magma creation requires an unusual heat to rise closer to the surface, an unusual drop in pressure, or an unusual pollutant (generally water) to enter the mantle and lower its melting temperature.*

Your worrisome situation in Pompeii can be blamed on the latter.

An intrusion of water into the mantle is the process responsible for many of the world's most powerful volcanoes. In slabs beneath oceans, water can infiltrate into their structure, and because water lowers a plate's melting temperature, this seemingly innocuous seepage is the first step of an incredibly volatile reaction that has led to some of the most catastrophic eruptions in history (see Krakatoa, 1883). In your case, the slab at fault is the sliver of the African plate below the Adriatic Sea, which slid (and indeed continues to slide) beneath the Eurasian plate along Italy's east coast.

When an oceanic plate with water in its structure submerges beneath a continental slab and dives toward the earth's warmer core, the weakened mantle melts and the lighter magma bubbles

---

*Water lowers the melting temperature of rock by weakening its chemical bonds. In other words, water does to rock what salt does to an icy road.

to the surface, liquefies the surrounding crust, and picks up new components. This doesn't always increase a volcano's destructive power, but as luck would have it Mount Vesuvius is located on a thick bed of limestone. Limestone ($CaCO_3$) plus heat results in the volcanically unfortunate combination of calcium oxide and CO_2. In other words, standing in Pompeii places you in the hazard zone of *carbonated* magma.

It gets worse. It so happened that after Vesuvius's previous eruption (believed to have occurred in 217 BCE), lava may have cooled somewhere in its piping system to create a plug. This plug probably delayed the next volcanic eruption by hundreds of years, but by doing so it dramatically increased the pressure building beneath the mountain, so that when the magma finally dislodged the rock, shook the earth, and exited the vent on the top of Mount Vesuvius, it did so with spectacular power.

As the lava depressurized, carbon dioxide and sulfuric gases rapidly came out of solution to create the magma-fueled jet engine, and the eruptive cloud of ash and gas rose in a formation called a Plinian column (named after Pliny the Younger, who documented the Vesuvius eruption from across the Bay of Naples). Mount Vesuvius's column rose more than twelve miles high, far above the cruising altitude of passenger jets.

But the trouble with the Mount Vesuvius eruption wasn't just its size. It was how many people lived so close. When I asked James Moore, a volcanologist and scientist emeritus at the U.S. Geological Survey, how best to survive an erupting volcano, he said it's quite easy: "Don't live near one!"

Yet that is more difficult advice to follow than it might seem. It wasn't just bad luck that the Romans built their city at the base of a volcano. Instead, volcanoes tend to attract human societies because their previous eruptions can produce nutrient-rich soils. If the Pompeiians had done any excavation, they might have found evidence of the massive Vesuvius eruption in 1995 BCE and the Bronze Age population it destroyed. But they didn't.*

As a result, you and the rest of the Pompeiians will find yourselves six miles from the vent of Vesuvius with only two options: Run north or run south.

If you run south and away from Vesuvius, it's a little unclear how far you'll need to go. We know that you'll need to run at least past the town of Stabiae—around four and a half miles away—because that was where Pliny the Elder (the Younger's uncle) died on the morning of the twenty-fifth. Second, if you run south, you'll also run in the direction of the prevailing winds, which means the Plinian cloud will continuously rain ash and pumice on you. At first, while the ash falls like snow, this may seem manageable. But as the eruption continues, the problem will only worsen. Eventually, the falling cloud will become so thick day will appear as night. In his notes Pliny the Younger described the darkness as "not so much a moonless or cloudy night, but as if the lamp had gone out in a locked room."

When I asked Petrone where the survivors of Pompeii went, he wrote that there's evidence of successful escapes to both north and south. However, he suggests you run north toward Naples—and toward the eruption. The road between Pompeii and Naples was well maintained, he explains, and the written records of those who survived suggest that most of the successful escapees fled north—while most of the bodies of the attempted escapees (who admittedly left far too late) were found to the south.

But if you do run north, you will need to move quickly, because you'll pass through the small Roman resort town of Herculaneum on your way to Naples—and Vesuvius's first pyroclastic surge flowed through Herculaneum.

*Or maybe they did and, like us, rolled the dice anyway.

Herculaneum sits barely four miles west of the volcanic vent, but for the first few hours of the eruption the prevailing winds largely spared it from most of the ash and pumice. But when Vesuvius first tapped into the deeper magma that triggered its initial pyroclastic flow, the heated gas and ash blew through Herculaneum and killed everyone there almost instantly.

Archaeologists have found scorch marks in the city that suggest the cloud may have been as hot as 930 degrees Fahrenheit when it engulfed Herculaneum's citizens. Because falling ash later encased the cloud's victims, archaeologists have been able to refill these spaces with plaster and re-create final poses that hint at the searing heat they experienced. These poses show almost no signs of the boxer-like defensive stance typically taken by victims of extreme heat, which suggests to Petrone that the Romans in Herculaneum died so quickly they never consciously registered discomfort. Petrone even found a glassy piece of brain matter in the skull of one Herculaneum victim, suggesting the cloud heated this person's brain so quickly it vitrified. If you don't want the same thing to happen to your brain, follow these instructions carefully.

Purchase your bread no later than 10 a.m. and exit Pompeii as soon as you see the black cloud. Luckily, the bakery conveniently puts you on the road to Herculaneum. All you'll have to do is head north.

Herculaneum is a little more than nine miles from Pompeii, and the pyroclastic flow doesn't hit until around 2 p.m. That gives you four hours, which means you can maintain the average walking pace of three miles per hour and arrive in Herculaneum just after 1 p.m.

Herculaneum was a beach resort town for the Roman elite. You'll find large, beautiful houses clad in marble and libraries filled with Ancient Greek and Roman classics. Some of these houses may seem like enticing places to wait out the troubles. But obviously, that would be a mistake.

Instead, you'll need to pass right through. If you want to be sure your brain remains unvitrified, you need to reach the outskirts of Naples—another four miles away. And to be extra safe, you should make it there within the hour, which means averaging a fast walk or jog.

The speed might seem manageable, but the total distance from Pompeii to Naples is thirteen miles. So, unless you're in extraordinary shape, you need to pace yourself. Avoid overexertion in the late-August heat and take any opportunity to drink fresh water. Crowds and obstacles may slow you down, but it might be surprisingly easy to get out of the city itself. At least if you leave quickly. Many residents initially take shelter, so you'll have an open window for your departure, which is critical for your survival. "Probably only those who managed to understand from the beginning the gravity of the situation escaped in time," Petrone told me. And perhaps to motivate any rubbernecking time travelers, he showed me a picture of the vitrified brain he found.

If you don't want that brain to be yours, don't stop, don't look around, and when you buy that bread, definitely get it to go.

HOW TO SURVIVE
THE SACK OF ROME

Let's say you want to visit the epicenter of a world power that somehow ruled a quarter of humanity across three continents for more than 500 years at a time when information could travel no faster than horseback. You want to see the famous sports arenas. The chariot races in the 150,000-seat Circus Maximus. The gladiators clash in the great Colosseum. You want to see the stolen art and treasures snatched by the tentacles of a Roman Empire, and at the end of the long day, you want to relax in some of their legendary public baths.

So you visit the city of Rome on August 24, 410 CE.

You'll walk the streets of Rome and see the wondrous architectural marvels. You'll see the Pantheon, the Arch of Constantine, the Aurelian Walls, and the Baths of Caracalla. You could catch a show at the Colosseum—more likely a "hunt" of an exotic animal rather than the rarer yet more famous gladiator battles. You might buy sausage or fried fish from the street markets. You'll drink wine in the taverns and maybe gamble a few denarii in a game of Roman dice. Then you might end your evening with a relaxing soak in the grand Thermae Alexandrinae, the legendarily luxurious public bathhouse built by Nero and renovated by Emperor Severus Alexander. Bathhouses were the Roman version of pork-barrel politics. Emperors commissioned them to appease the masses of their rule, which perhaps explains why the hated Nero built such a nice one. It was equipped with steam rooms, changing rooms, and heated rooms with open roofs. Its pools were fed by the bath's own dedicated aqueduct, its water warmed by a furnace burning wood chopped from its own dedicated forest, and all of it paid for by the bath's own dedicated tax. If you can find space in this popular bath, you can dunk in its cold pools, swim in its warm ones, or stew in its hot ones. And then sometime late that evening, perhaps just as you're nodding off in one of its soothing spas, you'll be startled by the long blast of a Gothic horn.

Rome may have at one time been an empire wealthy and powerful enough to construct this magnificent bathhouse, and the city may have at one time felt so confident in its power it didn't bother building walls. But that time has passed. In 271 CE, Rome began enclosing itself behind the twenty-six-foot Aurelian Walls—and on the night of August 24, 410 CE, 40,000 Visigoth soldiers rushed beyond them.

All empires fall, and you have arrived on the precipice of this one's oblivion. Over the next three days, Alaric and his Visigothic army will loot and pillage this once mighty global capital.

They will burn the Basilica Aemilia, steal the Solomon treasures from Jerusalem, torture Rome's senators, and kill its citizens. As Saint Jerome wrote in 416 of the sack: "The renowned city, the capital of the Roman Empire, is swallowed up in one tremendous fire; and there is no part of the earth where Romans are not in exile. Churches once held sacred are now but heaps of dust and ashes . . . It was as if the bright light of the world were put out."

The Visigoths seek gold and treasure, and the Thermae Alexandrinae sit next door to the Temple of Saturn, which serves as

Rome's treasury. So you need to leave. Quickly. The barbarians are coming and you only have a few minutes.

Grab a towel.

How exactly Rome fell from being an empire that once ruled a quarter of the world's population to one the Visigoths could siege and sack has been a topic of academic fascination for at least a thousand years and has been attributed to nearly as many causes.

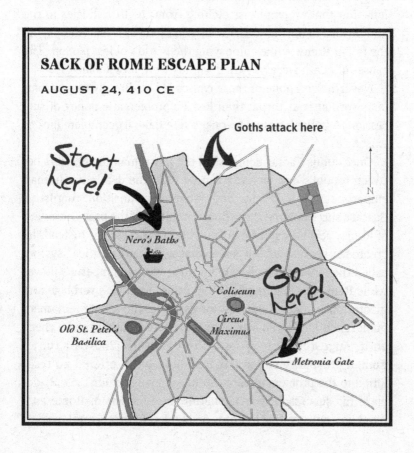

SACK OF ROME ESCAPE PLAN

AUGUST 24, 410 CE

Historians have alternately explained the fall as a result of everything from crushing taxes to an increasingly organized Gothic foe to a devastating series of plagues—even to mass lead poisoning. But as the Roman historian Edward Gibbon wrote in his seminal six-volume work, *The History of the Decline and Fall of the Roman Empire*, Rome's fall should not be seen as surprising or even particularly remarkable, because *all* empires fall.

Empires are complex, energetic political systems that always, inevitably falter. It's the social version of the second law of thermodynamics. The truly remarkable feature of Rome is not that it fell—but that an empire stretching from the British Isles to the Middle East to northern Africa lasted as long as it did. Autopsying the fall of Rome is like autopsying the world's oldest person. The causes of death were as varied as they were inevitable.

Nevertheless, none of those causes led so directly to a barbarian sword at your throat than Rome's problematic policy of succession. A policy plagued by one severe flaw: its complete lack of existence.

Once Julius Caesar demolished the few remaining barriers between republic and monarchy in 44 BCE, the death of a Roman emperor set off a delicate and dangerous transition. Augustus, Caesar's successor and the primary architect of the post-Caesar era of Rome, never established clear rules of succession. Instead, he created a successful but somewhat awkward political system called the Principate, wherein he ruled with an emperor's power while Rome retained much of the former republic's verbiage and institutions. Under Augustus, for example, the senate remained, but it functioned as an arm of his governance rather than a check on it. Augustus's Principate led to the nearly 200-year run of Roman prosperity called Pax Romana—but it offered no resolution to the problem of succession. Augustus couldn't simply declare his successor, lest he shatter the illusions of Rome as a republic, so instead he left only ambiguity. Rather than the eldest son inheriting the throne as in the later European kingdoms—which, for all its sexist and nepotistic faults, is at least a rule—Roman emperors came to power through some combination of backroom deals, violence, timing, and proximity. Even in relatively stable eras, this process resulted in a dangerous, deadly, ever more frequent series of coups. After the Roman emperor Nero committed suicide to avoid execution in 68 CE, his next three successors all died of assassination or suicide in a single year—and that was during an otherwise stable Roman era. After the so-called Crisis of the Third Century began in 235, when emperors discarded even the Principate's nods toward republicanism, the path to power ran through revolts, the military, assassination, and civil war.

The emperor's job was always dangerous, but in the Late Roman era it became almost ludicrously so. More than half of the fifty-nine emperors who ruled from 193 to 476 were either assassinated or executed, another four committed suicide, five died in battle, and—in an era when poisons were practically undetectable—many of the rest died with suspicious fevers. During the forty-nine-year Crisis of the Third Century, spanning from 235 to 284 CE, only two of the era's twenty-eight emperors died naturally. One would think this kind of job risk would discourage applicants, but the exact opposite occurred. Instead, emperors rerouted much of Rome's resources to gain and then stay in power. From 253 to 268, Emperor Gallienus fought six separate rebellions before he was finally assassinated.

The unsustainable turmoil at the top buckled the empire. In Rome's late period, it fought more than fifty civil wars, which killed far more Romans than the so-called barbarians. These civil wars created such an unquenchable thirst for troops that emperors began to recruit soldiers from beyond Rome's borders, including a man named Alaric who was from what is now Romania.

Alaric wasn't a Roman citizen, but he was at times a Roman

general, which was a common paradox in a Roman military that relied heavily upon foreign troops. He served in a role similar to a modern-day military contractor, alternately fighting either for or against Rome, depending on whether he had recently entered into a treaty or whether he was negotiating (i.e., ransoming) a new one.

On September 5, 394, after the Visigoths suffered heavy casualties fighting for the emperor Theodosius in his civil war against the usurper Eugenius, Alaric tore up his treaty with Rome and pursued a better one using the traditional Gothic negotiating strategy: He invaded.

Initially, he found some success. But after a new administration altered the deal, Alaric marched his Visigoths to the gates of Rome itself. He demanded to be named commander of Rome's western army, as well as land, food, and recurring payments for his soldiers. When the senators asked what he intended on leaving Rome's citizens if they refused, "their souls" was his only response. The emperor Honorius, safely tucked away in the city of Ravenna, declined Alaric's demands.

So, on the night of August 24, 410, those 40,000 Visigoths slipped through the Salerian Gate in the Aurelian Walls and put Rome to the sack.*

When Alaric's bugles blast out their triumph, they call out from the Salerian Gate in the city's far northeastern corner. This is good. You're in the Thermae Alexandrinae, a mile and a half from the breach, so you have some time before the Goths arrive.

Generally, the advice for surviving a sack is as simple as it is

---

*How exactly they made it past the wall has been a matter of debate since the day it occurred. Some accounts suggest a Trojan horse–like gambit from Alaric, some suggest treachery, and still others blame hunger or desperation from the Romans themselves.

imperative: Run! To an ancient sacking army, there was no distinction between citizens and soldiers. All were tortured, killed, or enslaved with equal impunity. This wasn't considered a war crime or even came as a surprise. It was simply expected. Medieval kings paid their armies with plunder—a payment that included the enslavement and freedom to commit acts of wanton brutality against a city that refused to surrender. Any life spared was a charity you would be ill advised to hope for.

Unfortunately, where exactly you should go is far less straightforward. The historical and archaeological record of the sack is scant, with only a few surviving sources and almost none that provide precise details. Even worse, the sources contradict one another. Where you should run, then, depends on who you believe.

If you believe the Christian philosophers Augustine of Hippo and Orosius, you will save yourself by escaping into a church. Alaric, as a Christian, took mercy on the Christian edifices and worshippers in the city, according to Orosius. He writes: "The Christian king Alaric went to great lengths to protect Christian buildings and treasures." The philosopher Augustine concurs, and even recommends a specific church: Old St. Peter's Basilica in what is now Vatican City. If he's correct, surviving the siege is fairly simple. The basilica is less than a mile to your west. If you move quickly, you can make it there before the Visigoths. Once inside, you can ride out their three-day pillage under Alaric's merciful protection.

But should you bet your life on these accounts? Perhaps not.

Almost immediately after the sack, the act itself became something of a political football between Europe's competing Christian and pagan factions. Rome had converted to Christianity in 323 CE, but plenty of its citizens still practiced paganism, and these pagans argued the sack was the gods' punishment for Rome's religious treachery. This created something of a conflict of interest among the Christian chroniclers, who now had incentive to emphasize the Christian Alaric's charity. Augustine himself admits as much in his *Retractions*: "Those who worship the multitude of false gods, whom we usually call pagans, tried to lay the blame for this disaster on the Christian religion . . . This fired me with zeal for the house of God and I began to write the City of God to confute their blasphemies and falsehood."

Perhaps Alaric's soldiers spared those who hid in churches, as Augustine claims, but his bias along with the few surviving clues from the archaeological record should give you some pause before you bet your life on it. The Basilica Aemilia, a church in the north of the city that Pliny the Younger once considered the most beautiful building in all of Rome, burned so hot in the sack that coins melted to its floor. Socrates Scholasticus, a Christian church historian in Constantinople, doesn't describe the sack in particularly peaceful terms, either. In 440 CE he wrote that "the barbarians . . . at last took Rome itself, which they pillaged, burning the greatest number of the magnificent structures and other admirable works of art it contained. The money and valuable articles they plundered and divided among themselves. Many of the principal senators they put to death on a variety of pretexts."

Scholasticus's account falls far more in line with the typical treatment of sacked cities in ancient and medieval times. So despite Augustine's and Orosius's claims, it seems you risk a significant chance of being treated according to the traditional medieval rules of war if you stay.

In other words, you should run.

The Goths pour into Rome from the north, so obviously you can't run there. You might think you should run away from them, to the south. But that probably isn't a good idea, either. If you run south, you'll run toward the Temple of Vespasian, which houses the legendary treasure from Jerusalem's Solomon Temple that the emperor Titus stole when he sacked the city in 70 CE (treasure that includes the Ark of the Covenant, if you believe some legends). The Goths loot the Solomon treasure, according to Procopius. You don't want to be in their way when they do.

So instead of running directly away from the invading army, you should head east, toward the Colosseum. You may even be able to see the top of the great arena from the street. Run toward it. As you go, take particular care to avoid Rome's wealthier districts like Palatine Hill and Aventine. The Goths torture the wealthy for information about their gold's whereabouts. If you travel through the poorer districts—generally the city's lowlands—you will not only see fewer soldiers, but those that you do see may be less inclined to torture you. Maybe.

Once you reach the Colosseum, continue east toward the Metronia Gate on the southeastern edge of the city. Unfortunately, it's unknown whether you'll find the gate open and unguarded. That detail has been lost. You'll just have to hope. But you do have history on your side, which suggests sacking soldiers usually rush in to gather their share of the spoils. If the Visigoth soldiers of fortune flood the city, you may find the gate open and the city unguarded. From there, you can wait out the sack in the safety of the surrounding hills.

Fortunately, the Sack of Rome is mercifully brief. The Visigoths are after gold; they're not occupiers. Once they grab every piece of wealth they can carry—and even some they can't, including a reported 2,000-pound silver cup—they continue south. After only three days, Alaric and his army leave and you can return to the city. You may even be able to continue your Roman vacation, because Alaric's invasion doesn't officially end the Roman Empire. It merely strikes the mortal blow. The Western Roman Empire stumbles on for another sixty years, during which time its population drops by 75 percent. In another 500 years, all of Rome can comfortably squeeze into the Colosseum's bleachers, and the disused arena will serve as a shantytown. Rather than fielding grand games, it will house cots, tents, and vagrants. By 1000 CE Rome takes on a certain *Planet of the Apes* vibe—a once massive and decadent city now sparsely populated and technologically defunct.

But that's not what you'll return to. Many Romans do survive, as do many of its buildings, including the Thermae Alexandrinae. You can go back. You'll find a little more space this time.

HOW TO SURVIVE

THE DARKEST YEAR OF
THE DARK AGES

L et's say you want to see the Dark Ages at their darkest. You want to peer into this opaque era for yourself and see what Europe was like after the Roman retreat. You want to see the Britons wage their titanic resistance against the invading Anglo-Saxons and investigate whether the mythical Briton leader King Arthur really existed and really killed 960 men in a single battle, as the legends claim. So you travel back to March 24, 536, to the hill fort of South Cadbury, one of the rumored sites for Camelot.

You see the vestiges of the Roman Empire: the Christian churches, the Roman roads and forts. You hear Latin still spoken by the city's elite, but Brittonic on its streets. You observe the ramparts, the huge dining hall, the knights and their horses. And sometime on that March day, you see the sun pass behind a cloud—and not emerge for nearly a decade.

You have arrived not only in the darkest year of the Dark Ages, but Harvard medieval historian Michael McCormick tells me he believes the year 536 to be the single worst year in human history.

* * *

On March 24, 536, a cloud obscured the sun and the earth plunged into thermal shock. Global temperatures dropped 5 degrees Fahrenheit. In the northern latitudes, they dropped by as much as 10. Tree ring analysis suggests the next decade was the coldest in 2,500 years. Snows fell in Baghdad. Blizzards raged through the summer in eastern China.

The perpetual cloud didn't merely chill the planet. It set off a series of dramatic feedback loops, reducing evaporation and dropping the planet into a global drought that shrunk the equatorial zone to a mere sliver. Few pieces of writing survive from this dark age, but what has suggests catastrophe across the entire Northern Hemisphere.

The Byzantine historian Procopius writes:

> The sun gave forth its light without brightness, like the moon, during this whole year, and it seemed exceedingly like the sun in eclipse, for the beams it shed were not clear nor such as it is accustomed to shed. And from the time when this thing happened men were free neither from war nor pestilence nor any other thing leading to death.

According to Roman senator Cassiodorus, 536 brought "a winter without storms, a spring without mildness, and a summer without heat." Michael the Syrian, author of the twelfth-century medieval *Chronicle,* wrote, "Each day the sun shone for about four hours, and still this light was only a feeble shadow. Everyone declared the sun would never recover its full light. The fruits did not ripen and the wine tasted like sour grapes." According to ancient Chinese records, a kingdom north of the Yellow River suffered such severe summer snows and droughts in 536, 537, and 538 that as much as 80 percent of the population died during the resulting famine. Archaeological evidence from the sixth century suggests villagers across Scotland, Ireland, and Scandinavia abandoned their farming communities entirely.

The cause of the cloud was a supermassive volcanic eruption, followed quickly by two more.

In an unprecedented series of volcanic activity, evidence from ice cores prove at least three different, massive volcanoes erupted in 536, 540, and 547 that combined to produce the greatest episode of atmospheric obfuscation in human history.

In 1783, Benjamin Franklin postulated that a volcanic eruption could alter global weather when he wondered whether Iceland's erupting Mount Hekla might be responsible for that year's persistent dry fog: "the rays of the sun . . . were rendered so faint in passing through it, that when collected in the focus of a burning glass, they would scarce kindle brown paper." In his reflection titled "Meteorological Imaginations and Conjectures," Franklin presciently went on to wonder whether it had happened before. "It seems however worth the inquiry whether other hard winters, recorded in history, were preceded by similar permanent and widely extended summer fogs," he wrote.

Three hundred years later, historians realized just how spectacularly correct he was. Though they had for centuries been aware of the written testimonies of the eyewitnesses to year 536, like Procopius and Cassiodorus, "we had largely dismissed them as hysterical," McCormick says. That began to change in the late 1990s when scientists analyzed ancient tree rings—the width of which they use to infer ancient climates—and discovered a remarkable consistency across the Northern Hemisphere: Beginning in the year 536 and continuing for the next decade, tree rings evidenced extreme growth anomalies. Not only did their widths testify to extremely poor growing seasons, they showed evidence of summer frosts.

Still, it wasn't until 2015, when analysis of ice cores showed a decade-long spike of sulfuric pollution that, McCormick explains, historians developed a consensus around the climatological catastrophe that occurred. The ash found in the ice cores chemically matched Icelandic rocks, which suggests that the cloud that darkened the sky that March day must have been a volcanic haze from an as yet undetermined caldera on that Atlantic island. The massive eruption blasted seventy cubic miles of ash and earth into the atmosphere and at least a hundred megatons of sulfur dioxide into the stratosphere. The ash and dirt fell to earth within weeks, but the sulfur dioxide combined with water to create tiny sulfuric acid aerosols. These droplets buffeted in the high winds of the stratosphere, creating a dry, sun-shielding volcanic haze that remained aloft for years. This fog reflected so much light that the sun shone with only 10 percent of its normal power in the mornings and evenings, according to anthropologist Joel Gunn, author of *The Years Without Summer: Tracing A.D. 536 and Its Aftermath.*

Then, four years later, it happened again.

In 540, a second volcano, this time somewhere closer to the equator—perhaps El Salvador's Ilopango—erupted in what was the largest blast of the past 7,000 years. While the 536 eruption primarily affected the Northern Hemisphere, Ilopango affected the entire globe. Seven years later, in 547, a third blast, believed to have occurred somewhere in Indonesia, again polluted the stratosphere with a sulfuric haze. Thanks to a series of poorly understood climatological feedback loops, the climatic cooling lasted for more than a century, but the severest effects occurred immediately.

Crops failed across the Northern Hemisphere. In northern Europe, the number of good growing days dropped by half. In Stockholm, the number of occupied sites fell by more than 75 percent. Farming villages became ghost towns. In southern Norway, the population fell by nearly half. The same pattern emerges in the archaeological record across what is now Denmark, Estonia, and northern Germany. The Irish *Annals of Inisfallen* note a "failure of bread" for the years 536 to 539. The Scots living in Ireland and the Picts of Scotland abandoned their farms entirely, relocated to the coast, and became fishermen. All archaeological and weather simulations suggest that in the decade following 536 northern Europe suffered one of the worst famines in recorded history.

Cities are particularly dangerous in medieval famines—and remember, you're in one of Britain's largest. You would think a sophisticated center of commerce and trade would insulate you from the famine compared to its effects on a rural farmer. You would be wrong.

At first, the local king (Arthur?!) distributed the grains he collected and stored in case of bad growing seasons. True famines were rare in the Early Middle Ages, but food shortages were common and a principal role for a king was to supply his people in times of dearth. Even in the best of times, farming in northern Europe was difficult and inefficient. Staple crop cereals like rye and wheat suffered a bad growing season every one year in four. There was no heavy plow, no crop rotation, and no proper fertilizer, so the average yield per seed of wheat sown was under four. Today, it's over forty.

In a large fort like South Cadbury, the king may have stored enough grain to sustain his people for a single bad year. But in medieval Europe, there were no resources nor the governmental sophistication to deal with extended dearth. In premodern times, no medieval society could store enough grain to last two consecutive bad years. So when the fog persisted and the year without summer stretched into the *years* without summer, Britons went from eating very little to eating the bark off trees.

Medieval cities like South Cadbury became death traps in famines. Urban residents relied on trade to feed themselves, and famines killed economies. As the food supply dwindled, the demand for what remained skyrocketed. Citizens had to reallocate everything they had toward purchasing what little food they could afford. As they did, demand for anything nonedible cratered. Cobblers, smiths, tailors, and the rest of the urban professions who drive city commerce lost their customers, jobs, and homes. Cities became impoverished.

Bringing food into the city in the best of times was already expensive. In sixth-century Britain, every fifty miles that a product had to travel over land doubled its price. In famine, that problem only worsened. When feed became too expensive, herders slaughtered their animals. Without refrigeration, Britons used salt to keep their meat. But at the same time demand for salt rose, the dimming sun reduced evaporation. Market specifics don't exist for the famine of 536, but in the medieval Great Famine of 1315 the price of salt quadrupled in less than a year when the drop in production combined with the increased demand. Without salt, excess meat goes to rot and dairies cannot produce their milk and cheese. With no demand for their product, tradespeople sold everything they owned for food, including their land. The very wealthy scooped up real estate at rock-bottom prices, while everyone else looked for work where there was none, and eventually ate food that wasn't really food.

When one year of fog turns into two, when crops fail for the second time, when your local grain stores run dry, you'll begin what historian William Chester Jordan calls the "strange diet" of medieval destitution. In the early stages of the famine, you'll eat animals that are not normally consumed, including, in rough order of descent: milking cows, ewes, horses, followed by pets and eventually rats. When the animals are gone, you'll begin to eat rotten food—perhaps not even knowingly. Desperate merchants may begin to pollute the food they sell with disgusting indigestible matter to make dwindling supplies last. In Paris during the

THREE VOLCANOES IN ELEVEN YEARS
DARKENED THE SKIES

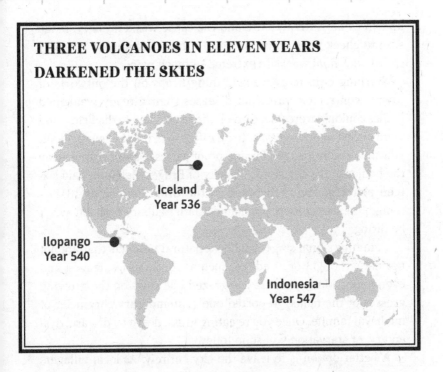

Iceland
Year 536

Ilopango
Year 540

Indonesia
Year 547

Great Famine, local bakers cut their product with wine dregs and pig droppings. (If you try to ride out the famine as a baker—don't do this. When the swindled townsfolk discovered the bakers' trickery, they tortured them.)

Once your diet descends to rotten matter, you've entered a dangerous stage. As tempting as rotten food may become, you should avoid it. In medieval famines rotten food killed more people than true starvation. Most died from parasitic diseases or dysentery that they contracted by eating diseased food. Villagers ate grain infested with fungi like ergot, which grows on rye after cold summers and causes excruciating intestinal pain followed by death. Today it's called ergotism, but in medieval times it was known as St. Anthony's fire and the cause was a mystery. Make sure to check your grain for signs of black fungus, or you may spend your final weeks in extreme stomach pain.

Starving citizens scavenged dung heaps on the outskirts of towns, contracted intestinal diseases their already weakened bodies couldn't overcome, died on the streets and in the fields, and were buried in mass graves. In an effort to maintain employment, you should consider the famine-proof profession of hauling away the bodies of the deceased. The city of Bruges, Belgium, paid sixteen pence per body disposed in the Great Famine of 1315—though the less densely populated South Cadbury probably won't be hiring.

In famine's final stage, you'll eat natural products that are not normally thought of as edible, such as roots, sprigs, leaves, and even bark. "Many paupers . . . grazed like cows on the growing grasses of the fields," reported one contemporary chronicler of medieval famine. Once you're eating grass, death by disease, dysentery, or starvation will soon follow.

A better option is to leave the city entirely. As local villagers watch their crops fail and they flock to the city, you should switch places with them. In the Great Famine, the rural villages fared far better than the urban areas. This seems counterintuitive, as cities would seem to provide safety in numbers. But it is exactly the opposite. In famines, density becomes dangerous. The smaller the community, the more easily you can survive off the land. While in the city you would be forced to eat whatever detritus you find on the street, in the villages you can supplement your diet with hunting and gathering. You might also have some success farming by adapting to the chill. When I asked Joel Gunn what you should plant, he suggested cold-resistant crops like rye or barley rather than emmer wheat.

Unfortunately, drought, cold, fog, and famine aren't the only reasons 536 is the worst year in human history. Instead, the cold has another, even more horrific effect.

High in the Tibetan Plateau, the chill and drought forced bubonic plague–carrying rodents into the more populated lowlands, where they infected traders. These traders ferried the plague west, and brought it with them in their boats down the Nile. In 541, the disease arrived in the Egyptian port city of Pelusium. From there, sea merchants spread it throughout the Mediterranean.

The novel bacterium exploded through the naive population. The plague hit Constantinople—the densely populated capital city of the Eastern Roman Empire—with particular fury. An estimated 30 percent of the city's more than half a million people died in the pandemic known as the Justinianic Plague. Once among the Romans and their ships, the disease spread throughout their vast trading network.

The archaeological record suggests the plague barely touched the Anglo-Saxons, probably because they didn't trade with the empires in the eastern Mediterranean, nor with anyone else on the mainland continent.

But the Britons did.

The Briton culture maintained a healthy trade with cities of the Eastern Roman Empire, who valued their copper and iron ore and exchanged it for fine Mediterranean wines and other luxury Roman goods. In all likelihood, *Yersinia pestis* traveled aboard one of these Roman trading ships and struck the killing blow the Anglo-Saxons couldn't. After centuries of stalemate, within a few years of the plague's arrival, the Anglo-Saxons swept across southern England, which had until recently been occupied and defended by powerful hill forts like South Cadbury. After famine and plague, these cities stood as shells of their former selves. One eighth-century Anglo-Saxon poem titled *The Ruin* describes the carnage their armies found in the Britons' forts:

> Days of pestilence came; death swept away all the bravery of men.
> Their fortresses became waste places; the city fell to ruin. The
> multitudes who might have built it anew lay dead on the earth.

To reiterate: You should leave the Briton city. All evidence suggests South Cadbury suffered a devastating annihilation. When the volcanic cloud passes in front of the sun, your only hope will be to abandon not only the cities but also the Britons. You need to commit the ultimate betrayal and take up with the enemy: the invading, Odin-worshipping, Old English–speaking Anglo-Saxons. You'll have to accustom yourself to their different ways. They live on simple family farms rather than in urban cities. They worship the same Germanic gods that inspired the Vikings, such as Thor, God of Thunder.

They do speak English, but that doesn't mean you'll understand them. Their ancient version is as different from modern English as German is today, so at best you'll pick out a word or two. But perhaps, with some practice, you may eventually speak it well enough to ask questions. Just don't ask them about King Arthur. That might be a touchy subject.

HOW TO SURVIVE

THE BLACK DEATH

Let's say you want to see a quintessential medieval city at the peak of its vitality. You want to see the pageantry of the courts, the knights, the shining armor, the jousts, the duels, the queens, kings, dukes, castles, and sieges. You want to see the Gothic architecture, the cathedrals, the painted frescoes, and the stained glass. So you travel back to London, England, on June 25, 1348.

You walk the city's crowded, muddy streets lined with spice shops, butcher shops, and goldsmiths. You stop by a tavern and enjoy a traditional medieval English meal of boiled bacon, bread, and a tankard of sweet, slightly alcoholic ale. You see the Tower of London and discover it looks almost exactly as it does in the modern day. You walk across the Old London Bridge and observe dozens of boats at port or sailing in and out with their shipments of wool, grain, vegetables, and fruit, all coming and going from European ports on the Atlantic and throughout the Mediterranean.

But while the sights and sounds of the medieval city may stagger, it's the smell that will hit you first: garbage, rotting meat, and human waste dumped on the road for the stray dogs, pigs, and rats to eat; the cadavers and decapitated heads of the traitors and thieves displayed on the city's walls; the stench of the sludge rivers and the sluice ponds flowing through the city's open-air plumbing.

When you travel to London in the early summer of 1348, you'll arrive in one of the loudest, smelliest, most violent, most polluted, and most powerful medieval cities in Europe. You'll also arrive at the very same time as another visitor to England. On June 25, 1348, a sickened sailor arrived into the port of Weymouth, 130 miles to your southwest. The name of the sailor has been lost, as has his port of origin—though it must have been from somewhere in the Mediterranean or perhaps northwest Spain. He might have arrived with symptoms as mild as a headache and cough. Or he may have been sicker. He may have been vomiting incessantly or, more tellingly, he may have arrived with large bulbous growths in his armpits or groin. Regardless, he likely died shortly after his arrival. But his fleas, and his disease, did not.

In an absolutely staggering piece of bad luck, you have arrived on the eve of what is perhaps the greatest catastrophe to ever befall humankind: the Black Death.

The Black Death was the world's first true pandemic, rivaled in its mortality and destruction only by the introduction of smallpox and measles to the New World. Until recently, many historians dismissed contemporary European accounts of the plague's mortality as hysterically hyperbolic. The evocations of mass graves and the deaths of entire neighborhoods seemed like the traditional exaggerations seen in accounts of historical battles. But more recent examination has suggested that, if anything, these were conservative and blinded to the truly global destruction of the plague. Tax records, payrolls, parish counts, and death certificates suggest that approximately half the entire populations of

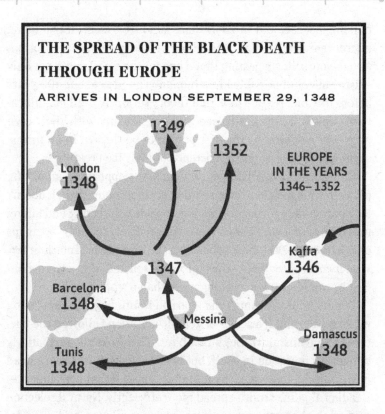

THE SPREAD OF THE BLACK DEATH THROUGH EUROPE

ARRIVES IN LONDON SEPTEMBER 29, 1348

1349

1352

EUROPE
IN THE YEARS
1346–1352

London
1348

Kaffa
1346

1347

Barcelona
1348

Messina

Damascus
1348

Tunis
1348

China, the Middle East, northern Africa, and Europe died from the disease. In just two years, at least 40 percent of the 100,000 people on the streets of London perished.

Yersinia pestis—the pathogen responsible for the disease alternately known as the plague, the bubonic plague, or simply the pestilence—is the most virulent bacterium ever known. It is a living organism, rather than a virus, which today often determines whether the pathogen is one modern medicine can destroy and one that it largely cannot. But in the medieval era, before antibiotics, it is a distinction without a difference. *Y. pestis* transmits between humans and animals. It rapidly replicates, causes horrific disease, and in 1348 there is no treatment. It is a living microorganism, though you should probably keep that information to yourself; suggesting that a bug far too small to see not only exists but could possibly kill a human is an idea about 400 years before its time. No one took that theory seriously until magnification allowed scientists to see microorganisms with their own eyes. You wouldn't be the first person to be thrown in an insane asylum for suggesting the existence of invisible creatures.

Underneath a microscope, *Yersinia pestis* appears as an oblong pill with what look like hairs swirling about its outer shell. It doesn't look particularly menacing, but it is capable of infecting and killing nearly anything with blood. It evolved relatively recently—perhaps only 5,000 or 6,000 years ago—from the innocuous bacterium *Yersinia pseudotuberculosis*, which grows in soil and, if you were to ingest it, would give you nothing more than a stomachache.

But at about the same time Pharaoh Khufu began constructing his Great Pyramid, a series of genetic mutations allowed the bacterium to transmit through flea bites. This wasn't a particularly dangerous mutation in itself, but because fleas must leave a dead host to find a new one, the mutation had a lethal consequence: Deadlier *Y. pestis* strains spread more efficiently. Natural selection pushed the bacterium toward increasing virulence, and in a Bacterial Big Bang—a stomach bug morphed into a monster.*

The process of infection begins when a flea feeds on a septicemic animal—usually a rodent. Once the flea bites an infected animal, the bacteria grows into a giant brown mass within the

---

*One particularly lethal evolution seems to have been a chemical secretion that steals iron from the host that the bacteria needs to fuel its furious replication. This secretion is so critical to its lethality that modern researchers working with *Y. pestis* render the bacteria harmless merely by disabling it. However, in one tragic case from 2009 that otherwise exemplifies the importance of iron acquisition for the bacteria, a researcher with an undiagnosed hereditary disease causing his body to overproduce iron contracted the attenuated strain and died.

flea's gut and blocks the flea's esophagus. The blocked flea eventually starves to death, but not before it hunts for new hosts in a ravenous blood frenzy. When it finds one and inserts its feeding tube beneath its victim's skin, the blood mixes with the brown pathogenic mass and the flea regurgitates the blood-bacteria mixture back into its victim, injecting between 25,000 and 100,000 *Y. pestis* bacteria directly into the bloodstream.

The immune system rallies to action when it detects any flea bite, sending a battery of white blood cells to investigate and destroy any foreign invaders introduced by the breach. Epidemiologists once believed *Yersinia pestis* somehow hid from these white blood cells, but recent research suggests it instead kills them by injecting a toxin via a needle-like protrusion. When immune cells responsible for surrounding and removing dead cells consume these destroyed white blood cells, they become infected themselves and flush to the nearest lymph node, where the bacteria begins its furious growth.

Once inside the host via flea bite, the disease proceeds down one of two paths. A third of the time, the pathogen directly infects the blood. In these cases, the patient never develops the characteristic lymph buboes, and, instead of a delayed symptomatic onset, the patient sickens almost immediately. Their blood soon teems with bacteria, they become extremely infectious, and death is certain.

In the more common form of the disease, *Y. pestis* asymptomatically replicates within the lymph nodes for the first three-to-five days before it seeps into the bloodstream and symptoms begin. The infection often announces itself with a fever and a headache, though both are mild enough to be confused with the flu. The characteristic symptoms of the bubonic plague begin with the appearance of a red ring around the flea bite, followed by the enormous swelling of the lymph nodes closest to the bite. Eventually, the ring turns gangrenous, and the pustules burst with blood and pus. Fever, chills, and headache progress to nausea, incessant vomiting, diarrhea, and severe abdominal pain. The case fatality rate for this form of the disease is 60 percent, and death, if it occurs, usually follows a week after the onset of symptoms.

Less commonly, the infection transmits person to person, either through bodily fluids or—more dangerously—through the air. If the infection progresses to the lungs, every exhalation, laugh, or cough ejects millions of bacilli into the air within flecks of microscopic spittle. Breathing in *Y. pestis* directly infects the lungs and is universally fatal.

But as well as the plague spreads through humans, we are not its natural hosts. Instead, rodents, particularly those living in high and dry climates, provide the natural reservoir. The plague is believed to have first emerged somewhere in the Tibetan Plateau, perhaps from a gerbil population in the mountainous regions of Pakistan. After its first outbreak in 541—called the Plague of Justinian—it had remained relatively isolated in these mountains until the fourteenth century.

Michael McCormick, a professor of medieval history at Harvard, tells me that no one knows why the Black Death broke out when it did. However, because most modern plague outbreaks occur after a severe drought craters rodent populations and sends their fleas hunting for new hosts, he suspects a meteorological trigger. Whether it was rain, drought, a cold summer, or just bad luck, what is known is that in the mid-fourteenth century the plague burst out of the mountains and infected traders following the Silk Road. From there, the plague moved east into China and west to the Mediterranean.

In 1346, while sieging the Crimean port city of Kaffa, Mongol soldiers began to die of a new disease. Gabriele de' Mussi, a fourteenth-century Italian notary, wrote that they suffered from a "mysterious illness that caused swelling in the armpit or groin and a putrid fever . . . All medical advice and attention was useless; the

Tartars died as soon as the signs of disease appeared on their bodies . . . The dying Tartars, stunned and stupefied by the immensity of the disaster brought about by the disease . . . lost interest in the siege. But they ordered corpses to be placed in catapults and lobbed into the city in the hope that the intolerable stench would kill everyone inside."

The hungry fleas on the bodies of these early biological bombs killed Kaffa citizens far more efficiently than any army. Genoese traders abandoned the plague-ridden port but carried the pathogen within their bodies and in the rats on their ships to the Sicilian city of Messina in October 1347. From there, it spread throughout Italy, Europe, northern Africa, and the Middle East.

On June 25, 1348—eighteen months after Mongol soldiers launched their dead over the walls at Kaffa—the plague crossed the English Channel in the body of a sailor.

On September 29, it appeared in London.

The timing should have been lucky. Fleas are most active in the heat of summer, so European cities with summer introductions suffered significantly worse death rates than those in other seasons. Unfortunately, the London winter of 1348 happened to be warm and humid. The fleas kept biting, and Parliament declared an emergency by January. In the sixty days comprising February and March, 20 percent of the city died.

To save yourself, you might think you should postpone your urban tour and leave the city for a smaller countryside village. You might think you can escape the plague if in September you depart the density and detritus of London for one of the many farms ringing the city. But while this would be a wise choice for most pathogens, human density does not dictate bubonic plague's spread. Instead, it's the density of rats and fleas to humans that matters. The result is that a seemingly safe small farm or village is actually more dangerous thanks to a larger rat-to-human ratio. In rural towns, the arrival of the plague cratered the rat population and sent thousands of hungry, infected fleas hunting for meals among few human hosts. The likelihood you get bit in this scenario actually increases compared to the denser cities, which explains why the rural mortality of the plague in England exceeded that of its cities. The only reason you should run from the city is if you have access to a wealthy landowner's relatively ratless countryside villa. So either make wealthy friends or stay put in the city.

There are safer districts within London, however.

Tax records suggest citizens living in the south of the city suffered slightly lower death rates than those in the north. That was probably because, like most epidemics, the Black Death hit the poor harder than the wealthy. The denser housing and dirtier streets of the northern districts attracted more rats than the rest of the city. However, the gap in the death rates between the wealthy and the poor in the first wave wasn't nearly as wide as is often seen in pandemics, or even what occurred in later waves of the plague. The demographics of those buried suggest what archaeologists call a "catastrophic mortality profile," or a disease that killed indiscriminately, regardless of wealth or class, as if a bomb had detonated on the city. Elites died alongside the poor, including at least three archbishops as well as King Edward III's own daughter Joan. Ignorance nullified many of the typical advantages afforded the elite in the initial outbreak. Without knowing how or why the disease spread, the wealthy couldn't deploy their money or influence to save themselves. In subsequent waves, London's elite fled to their villas and suffered far less than those who couldn't afford to. But in the first wave, devastation swept across social classes, and the medical care the wealthy could afford afforded no help at all.

Medieval medical philosophy still relied on Galen's second-century theory of humors, which posited that sickness resulted from an imbalance of bodily fluids. If you see a physician—which you shouldn't—they may prescribe a course of bloodletting or lance your buboes and produce nothing more than considerable pain. They may also prescribe other, stranger remedies. Some doctors, for instance, believed placing a chicken's genitals over the buboes provided a cure.

Obviously, given the available medical care, you need to concentrate on your defense from infection. First, wear a mask around other people, particularly other sick people. Pneumonic plague spreads through the air—though, because those with septicemic or pneumonic plague will be very sick, you're only likely to encounter it if you're caring for a sick patient.

Contracting plague via flea bite is both more likely and more difficult to defend against, because isolating yourself from others won't be sufficient. You also need to isolate yourself from rats. That means removing anything rats might eat or use for a home, including brush, rock piles, trash, and excess firewood. You might think you should get a cat. You shouldn't. The only thing more dangerous than a live rat is a dead one. The fleas on a dead host scatter, probably onto you or your cat.*

To prevent their bites, cover up as much skin as possible. Wear long-sleeved shirts and pants. Tuck in your shirt and your pant legs into your socks. Check yourself for fleas frequently, wash your hands with soap, and bathe regularly. Local doctors believe "spore-opening" activities like bathing provide an entrance for the disease, so they advise Londoners against the practice. Do the opposite. Bathe often and encourage those around you to do the same. Consider complaining loudly of their smell. But even if you manage to avoid infection, you'll feel the effects of the disease everywhere.

---

*If you do have a cat, the CDC specifically recommends not to sleep in bed with it. According to the CDC info sheet, sharing a bed with a pet "has been shown to increase your risk of getting plague."

The plague touched every aspect of European life. In rural areas, harvests went uncollected. As crops rotted in the fields, food shortages led to rampant inflation. Trade in London, which relied on the production of goods outside the city, was almost completely severed. The economy stagnated to such a degree that ice cores show a dramatic fall in the air's lead pollution as Europe smelted fewer coins during the four-year Black Death.

As the plague stretched on, the streets of London became a mortuary. Mass graves, dug in preparation, filled five bodies deep. The sense of despair that must have accompanied a catastrophe of this magnitude seems beyond any modern comparison. The author Daniel Defoe, who chronicled his experiences living through a resurgence of the 1665 London plague in *A Journal of the Plague Year*, wrote: "London might well be said to be all in tears . . . The shrieks of women and children at the windows and doors of their houses, where their dearest relations were perhaps dying, or were just dead, were so frequent to be heard as we passed the streets, that it was enough to pierce the stoutest heart in the world to hear them."

If your summer arrival in the medieval capital feels like entering a new world—by winter, it'll feel like the end of one. What had just a few months before been a thriving city will devolve into an apocalyptic ghost town populated by the mourners, the dead, and the dying. In his journal of the Black Death, one Irish monk conveyed what must have felt like a true possibility when he wrote that he only maintained his chronicles "in case anyone should still be alive in the future."

But the pandemic did end. By the late fall of 1349, just over a year after the first infected person arrived in London, the case numbers waned, and by winter, through a combination of a decimated rat population, fewer fleas, and a highly immunized population, the pandemic ended after killing nearly half of London in just eighteen months.

Then a miraculous thing happens. If you survive by tucking

away in the northern half of the city or in some rat-free manor in the countryside, then by the spring of 1350 you should emerge or return. Because the city, though devastated, is on the verge of a remarkable, near-inexplicable recovery. The end of the Black Death left streets empty of shoppers and fields bereft of farmers, yet rather than leave a wake of economic destruction, other than the industrial revolution it produced the greatest increase in living standards over the past 2,000 years. Overnight, mass death and suffering transitioned to mass prosperity. Demand for labor spiked, wages tripled, income inequality plunged, and the combination finally sank England's oppressive system of serfdom. In a medieval economy based largely on fixed resources like productive growing lands, metals in the ground, or coastal access, fewer people meant more for everyone. Prior to the industrial revolution, density decreased prosperity. The size of medieval Europe's Malthusian economic pie was fixed. Territories generated wealth almost entirely from whatever they could grow, shepherd, or remove from the sea. An increase in population did not lead to more grazing or productive agricultural land. Instead, an increase in population simply split the economic pie into smaller pieces. Prior to the Black Death, the swelling population led to damaging, life-threatening degrees of competition over land, jobs, and food. Workers had less bargaining power, their wages stagnated, and wealth concentrated at the top in the powerful system of feudalism.

The day the Black Death arrived, nearly 50 percent of England's population lived as serfs. They didn't own the land they worked and they owed most of their production to their lord. They couldn't leave their land for longer than a day, were restricted in who they could marry, and had almost no chance of earning the consistent profit that might have allowed them true landownership. Instead, the lord owned the land and everything on it, while serfs, it was said, "owned nothing but their own bellies."

The Black Death changed that. The collapse of the population increased the bargaining power of the remaining workers to such a degree that in 1349 the wealthy, property-owning members of Parliament passed the Statute of Labourers Law, which capped a worker's wages to pre-plague levels and prohibited rural farmers from seeking higher wages in cities. It was to no avail. Henry Knighton, a clergyman in Leicester during the Black Death, wrote that peasants "took no notice of the King's command . . . If anyone wanted to hire them he had to submit to their demands, for either his fruit and standing corn would be lost or he had to pander to the arrogance and greed of the workers."

In Rochester, another contemporary chronicler wrote, "There was such a shortage of servants, craftsmen, and workmen, and of agricultural workers and labourers . . . that the humble turned up their noses at employment, and could scarcely be persuaded to serve the eminent unless for triple wages." In 1400, serfs dropped to 35 percent of the population; by 1500, they were all but gone.

In Russia and eastern Europe, the landowning elite successfully colluded to keep the wages and living standards of the proletariat depressed, and the Black Death resulted in little social change. But in western Europe, the drop in income disparity and increase in wages had far-reaching effects. Higher labor demand drew more women into the workforce, which increased the average marrying age and decreased the average family size, lowering the rate of population growth, which, in a Malthusian economy, created a longer ascent of living standards. Wages in coastal cities like London that sat at the center of trade rose faster and recovered more quickly than those of interior cities such as York. Their rise in prosperity allowed them to invest in infrastructural improvements and gain a productivity advantage that never relented.

Remarkably, in a city that just lost half its population, the future is far brighter than it has any reasonable right to be. Somehow, if you can survive and endure a rather bleak eighteen months, you might find the vivacious medieval vacation you came for.

HOW TO SURVIVE

THE FALL OF
CONSTANTINOPLE

Let's say you want to read some of Johannes Gutenberg's first printed words as they come off the press. You want to watch the ink dry on some of the first sentences produced by a technology that democratized knowledge, inspired an unprecedented surge in literacy, pushed Europe into the modern age, and didn't invent a new means of communication so much as invent mass communication.

So you travel back to the year 1453, to the town of Mainz, Germany, and you search for Gutenberg and his press. When I ask Cornelia Schneider, curator at the Gutenberg Museum, where to look, she tells me you can find his workshop in a big house called Hof zum Humbrecht, which is just a few blocks north of the Mainz Cathedral along the banks of the Rhine. There you'll observe Gutenberg invent a printing technique that remained the standard for almost 500 years. Watch as he carefully sets two pages of Gothic-printed letters over the course of six hours, smacks them with ink, and then presses the letters against paper until his entire contraption creaks under the strain. If you pick up one of the sheets, you can settle into a corner and read one of the first ink-stamped pages.

You may at first be a little surprised at what you see, because you won't be reading a page from the famous Gutenberg Bible. His Bible is his most renowned work—and for good reason. The 180 copies he printed using his efficient press revolutionized communication by dramatically cutting the cost of producing books, leading to a democratization of both their knowledge and even literacy itself. But before he could print the Bible, Gutenberg needed to test his device and he needed to raise money, explains Eric White, curator of rare books for the Princeton University Library and author of *Editio Princeps: A History of the Gutenberg Bible*. To do so, Gutenberg printed a variety of smaller contract jobs. He printed a German poem, a few Latin grammar books—but he also printed a plea written by the Catholic Church.

So if you visit Gutenberg's printing press in 1453 and read one the first documents ever printed, you'll read an ad.

It's a call for a crusade.

The ad was an effort by the Catholic Church to raise money and recruit soldiers for a new offensive against the Sultan Mehmed II and his expanding Ottoman Empire. The twenty-one-year-old Mehmed II had been sultan for only two years, but he had already marshaled his forces to Constantinople's doorstep. Without the eastern capital of Christianity serving as a bulwark, the Church feared the Islamic onslaught would continue all the way to western Europe, so they fell back on a centuries-old strategy to stem it: They tried to raise a crusade.

It didn't work.

According to White, the world's first print advertising campaign failed spectacularly. By the fifteenth century, European citizenry had lost their crusading appetite. Enthusiasm for starvation marches to engage in combat with edged weaponry had long since dimmed. But even when the Church merely asked for funds, rather than lives, it found a cynical audience. For too many years the Vatican had used the specter of an Islamic onslaught to raise money for foreign fights and then used it to line local pockets. As Pope Pius II later lamented, "People think our sole object is to amass gold. No one believes what we say. Like insolvent tradesmen, we are without credit."

For Gutenberg, the medium was a resounding success, but his first message a spectacular failure. Almost no European money or soldiers ever went to the aid of Constantinople as it prepared for its existential battle against the Ottoman Empire.

But you're not as jaded as the medieval European public, so let's say you buy the pitch, and you go to the defense of the city. You sail down the Italian coast, through the Mediterranean, past Greece, into the Aegean Sea, then the Sea of Marmara, up the Bosporus Strait, into the Golden Horn, and in the spring of 1453 you arrive at the capital of the Byzantine Empire.

You're sailing into a slaughter.

Outside the city, 80,000 soldiers of the Ottoman Empire prepare for siege. Leading the army is the Sultan Mehmed II, whose ambition is only matched in size by a nose so large and crooked that one portrait artist later described it as "on point of touching his lips." When his father, Murad, died, Mehmed ordered his baby brother drowned to clear up any issues of successorship.* Then he mobilized his empire to take Constantinople. All his life,

---

*Mehmed II believed so fervently in fratricide that he not only formalized the practice into law, but recommended that whichever of his many sons became sultan should kill the rest of Mehmed's own children "in the interest of the world order." His son Bayezid gruesomely took his advice and ordered nineteen of his siblings strangled in a single night. Some historians also believe that Bayezid poisoned Mehmed himself, who died of a sudden illness at age forty-nine.

he later said, he'd dreamed of making the city the capital of the Ottoman Empire and fulfilling the prophecy Muhammad himself had set forth when he said: "One day Constantinople will be conquered. Great is the commander who conquers it. Great are his soldiers."

In the two years since he became sultan, Mehmed marshaled the vast resources of the Ottoman Empire toward his goal. He constructed an entire castle—the Boğazkesen (literally "throat-slitter")—at the narrowest point of the Bosporus Strait for the sole purpose of blocking aide to Constantinople. Then he hired a Hungarian specialist to build him the world's greatest cannon. Known as the Basilic, it was not only the largest artillery piece at the time; it is one of the biggest cannons ever constructed. Cast entirely in bronze and measuring 24 feet long, it could fire a 600-pound cannonball over a mile. Yet it wasn't the most practical device. The barrel required three hours to cool before it could be fired again, and at 35,000 pounds it was so heavy it required 60 oxen and 400 men to move. But Mehmed II's preparations hardly stopped at artillery. He constructed at least 60 ships, hired mercenaries, and trained an army of at least 80,000 soldiers.

On April 6, 1453, he gathered his cannons, ships, and soldiers at the walls of Constantinople.

But what walls they were.

Constantinople (called Istanbul today) is a natural fortress. The city sits on the point of a peninsula jutting into the Sea of Marmara, poking out into the confluence of the Golden Horn inlet that runs along the city's north edge and the Bosporus Strait to its east. Deep water envelops the city on three sides, and along this entire sea-facing frontage rose stone walls fifteen to thirty feet high. On the fourth side, along the city's land-exposed western flank, rose the great Theodosian Walls. Built by Emperor

Theodosius II in 413, they formed the most formidable defensive structure in Europe.

The Theodosian barricade was not a singular wall, but instead a series of three. The first wall was a six-foot-high sheer stone barrier, which stood behind a sixty-foot-wide, thirty-foot-deep moat. Behind the small wall towered a thirty-foot-high, fifteen-foot-thick outer wall, and behind *that* loomed a sixty-five-foot-tall interior wall, which was anchored on both ends with fortresses and interspersed with no fewer than ninety-six regularly spaced, thirty-foot-high towers.

Emperor Theodosius built this ridiculously imposing defensive structure because the city's pivotal location along land and sea trading routes, as well as its natural deep-sea port, had inspired envy and attack for more than a thousand years. Mehmed II was not the first emperor to covet Constantinople's throne, nor the first Ottoman sultan, nor even the first in his family. In 1422 his father had sieged the city for three months, assailed the walls with 10,000 soldiers, and failed. The Slavs attacked and failed in 540, 559, and again in 581. In 626, 12,000 Constantinople defenders defeated an army of 80,000 Persian and Avar soldiers, and from 669 to 679 Arab attackers led a near-sustained siege on the city. That too failed. Constantinople's massive fortifications enabled the city to survive nearly every attack save for an assault by Christian Crusaders in 1204, who sieged and sacked the city before the Byzantines regained control.

But even the tallest walls require defenders, and by the time you sail into Constantinople, the Byzantine Empire will have long passed its former glory. At their height more than a millennium ago, the Byzantines—who called themselves the Eastern Roman Empire—conquered the Mediterranean. Their territory stretched from present-day Spain to Jerusalem to northern Africa. You'll see the former wealth and opulence of their empire in the magnificent buildings, art, and libraries around the city. These buildings include the Hagia Sophia, built in the sixth century, which at 180 feet tall stood for a time as the tallest building in the world. You'll see the great Hippodrome, the arena built in the third century to host the city's giant chariot races; it seats as many as 100,000 spectators—more than twice that of Rome's Colosseum.

The Byzantine Empire was once the most powerful in the region—and perhaps the world—but a millennium of famine, plague, and the rising Ottoman Empire whittled it down to a fraction of its former glory. By the time you arrive, the empire that had once conquered the Mediterranean will barely control its own peninsula. Where once the empire could draw upon resources from across three continents to defend itself, when Mehmed and 80,000 soldiers march into view of the parapets, the city can muster only a mere 7,000* to its defense.

Join that defense, but do so wisely. The seawalls, which stand between fifteen and thirty feet tall and surround the city's ocean frontage, see the least combat, and thus are the safest assignment. Unfortunately, it's more likely you'll be posted on the Theodosian Walls themselves, where the Ottomans focus their attack. Even so, some sections of this wall will be more dangerous than others. If you can, avoid a deployment in the middle section, called the Mesoteichion—it's where the Lycus River runs, where the walls are weakest, and thus where Mehmed concentrates his assault. Try to guard the northern or southern edges of the wall instead. From there, you'll watch as the Ottoman army establishes its camps, sails its ships into the Bosporus Strait, and marshals its massive artillery into position.

On April 6, 1453, you'll see a large puff of smoke rise from the

*7,001 counting you.

Basilic cannon. You'll hear a mighty, distant boom and feel the parapets shudder from the impact of its 600-pound stone ball.

The Theodosian Walls weren't built with cannons in mind, so when the 600-pound rock balls slam into the barriers, the stones crumble and shatter. Nevertheless, the outer wall is more than thirty feet thick. Some of the shots bring down sections, but you and the rest of the defenders can scurry down at night and in between volleys fill the gaps with wood, dirt, and pieces of shattered stone before any Ottoman force can organize an attack. With continuous repair, the walls hold.

On April 12, after six days of relentless bombardment, the Ottomans launch their first frontal assault. The battle may at first feel definitive, but Mehmed is merely probing. At this early stage he's not yet committed to sending the weight of his full army. Instead, he's testing the will and defensive tactics of the city and its lead defender, a Genoese warrior and part-time pirate named Giovanni Giustiniani. Don't worry. It's a test the city easily passes.

The Ottomans concentrate this assault in the gaps formed in the partially shattered sections of the wall, but in those narrow paths their numerical advantage means nothing. Ground troops fight their frontal lines to a standstill, while you and the rest of the defenders atop the wall can assail the invaders with arrows, rocks, bullets from handheld cannons (called culverins), spears, and boiling oil. Some attackers attempt to climb the walls with ladders and grappling hooks, but you can chop the ropes, push away the ladders, and engage the unfortunate few that arrive on top. After four hours of fighting, the Ottomans suffer heavy casualties while inflicting few, and retreat. With any luck, if you remain on top of the interior wall, you should be safe.

His land attack foiled, Mehmed tries again, this time by sea. As it has done for centuries it its defense, the city will extend a massive chain across the mouth of the Golden Horn inlet to prevent attacking ships from surrounding the city's coastline, then will defend the chain with its navy.

Though Mehmed's ships outnumber Constantinople's, the city's navy is the superior one, and in the first sea battle the Ottomans suffer another severe defeat. On April 20, four European ships even manage to slip past the Ottoman blockade and provide the city with much-needed aid. But in a move of tactical genius, Mehmed rolls his naval fleet overland on oiled logs, circumventing Giovanni's blockade.

Don't take part in these sea battles if you can avoid it—and if you can't, don't be captured. The Ottomans gruesomely torture and execute all sixty sailors they take prisoner. In response, the Byzantines march all 260 of their Ottoman captives to the top of the wall and behead them.

The loss of control over the Golden Horn is a blow to the Constantinople defense, but not a mortal one. Over the next month, every Ottoman tactic and assault ends in disaster. On May 7 they again assault the walls, this time by filling in the moat with dirt and debris and rolling giant wooden towers to the wall. But this seemingly ingenious plan will end disastrously when soldiers from Constantinople slip out at night with sacks of black powder and detonate the massive structures. If you need to prove your bravery after your sea battle dereliction, you can join this group. They make it home.

After Mehmed's plan to go over the top of the walls fails, he orders his army to go below. His miners dig tunnels beneath the walls, seeking both to destabilize them from underneath and to sneak soldiers behind their lines. But this attack fares even worse than the towers. Constantinople counters with its own tunnels. They intercept the unfortunate miners they encounter and torture them for the locations of the other tunnels. When they find them, they fill them with fire and smoke.

By May 25, after a month and a half of successful defense, you may begin to feel like you might survive. You might believe that the city will once again hold. Even Mehmed himself apparently has doubts, because he offers a deal. He guarantees the lives and possessions of every citizen of Constantinople if Emperor Palaiologos surrenders the city.

But Palaiologos declines, and Mehmed decides his only option is to pursue a final, all-out assault. Spies in the Turkish camp report Mehmed's decision back to Constantinople, and both sides prepare for the deciding battle.

The Ottoman army spends Saturday, May 28, resting and praying, while in Constantinople the city fills the Hagia Sophia for an enormous ceremony.

You'll have very little time left in Constantinople, but when Mehmed rests his army it gives you a few free hours. You need to spend them wisely. You need to salvage Constantinople's most valuable possessions.

You need to save its books.

The thousand-year-old Imperial Library of Constantinople was at one time one of the best-stocked libraries in the world, housing more than 100,000 manuscripts from the Ancient Greek philosophers, many of which were the world's only copy. These books were more than just intellectual curiosities or valuable artifacts. In a medieval Europe that had long forgotten the knowledge of the Ancient Greeks, these timeless works contained the revolutionary philosophies that would provide the catalyst for the Renaissance. The word "Renaissance" comes from the French word for "rebirth" because the intellectual movement was sparked not by new ideas, but the rediscovery of very old ones.

As Constantinople stood on the verge of collapse, Europe hungered for the ideas and discoveries of the Ancient Greeks and Romans. This interest began more than a century earlier, when the

Italian poet Petrarch—considered the "father" of the Renaissance—found a series of long-forgotten letters between the Ancient Roman statesman Cicero and his childhood friend Atticus discussing the ideas of the Ancient Greek philosophers. These letters set off a movement among medieval scholars to rediscover the books of the Ancient Greek and Roman philosophers. They dragged Europe out of what Petrarch called his era's "Dark Ages" and sparked the greatest intellectual revolution in Europe's history.

The books of the Ancient Greeks sitting in Constantinople and moldering away in European monasteries contained philosophies and scientific discoveries of almost unimaginable genius, far more advanced than those of Europe's scientists living more than a thousand years later. They included the theories of scholars like Democritus, who in 400 BCE came to the remarkable conclusion that humans, the earth, the sky, and everything else in the universe were composed of tiny individual particles that combined to form an infinite arrangement of complex structures. He called these particles "atoms."

The books contain the even more radical ideas of the Ancient Greek philosopher Epicurus, who built on Democritus's ideas and reasoned that if the universe was built upon atoms and void, then humans occupied no more special a place in the universe than any other creature or matter. If there was no hierarchy of material, he argued, then humans, the stars, and the sun could not be supreme celestial beings. Instead, they were simply transitory collisions of atoms: born from nothing and destined for the void. But rather than spark an existential crisis, Epicurus believed this knowledge to be wonderfully freeing. It freed him from the burden of pleasing the gods or sacrificing for them in some hopeless attempt to win their favor. It freed him to seek that which made him happy, to pursue scientific discovery, and to avoid pain and suffering. If there was nothing to be gained from pain, suffering served no purpose.

In a medieval era dominated by Church orthodoxy that

considered pleasure-seeking behavior a sin, suffering a path to salvation, and discouraged scientific inquiry that pried into "God's secrets," Epicurus's ideas were profound, controversial, and infectious. They sparked a philosophical movement called Humanism, which became the driving philosophy behind the Renaissance. Humanism radically realigned European philosophy and science by placing agency on the self, rather than in the divine or supernatural. Humanists were not necessarily atheists. In fact, most of them were devout Roman Catholics. But they centered the pursuit of happiness, sought rational explanations for earthly problems, and shifted their focus to humans, rather than the divine. Famous Humanists include many of the Renaissance's most celebrated philosophers and thinkers, including Giordano Bruno (later burned at the stake), Niccolò Machiavelli, and Leonardo da Vinci.

At the same time that western European interest in the works of the Ancient Greeks began to grow, refugees fleeing Constantinople brought the means to fertilize them. They carried books and the language to read them. Among these refugees was the scholar John Argyropoulos, who survived the sack of Constantinople and escaped to Florence, where he went on to translate numerous Ancient Greek texts and teach classical Greek to students—including Leonardo da Vinci—before he died in Rome in 1487 (supposedly from overconsumption of watermelon).

You need to help him.

You can join the refugees in Italy who dump fuel on the sparks of western Europe's Humanist movement and help drive profound revolutions in science, politics, and art that reverberate to the modern day. You just need to save a few books first.

You can find the library near the entrance to the palace (see map). When you make your way inside, look for works that scholars know existed but have never been found, such as most of the books of Diogenes (you'll see it written as Διογένης), Homer's (Ὅμηρος) first poem, Aristarchus of Samos (Ἀρίσταρχος) and his wild theory that the Earth and planets orbit the sun, along with most of the writings of Aristotle (Ἀριστοτέλης).

You have until midnight.

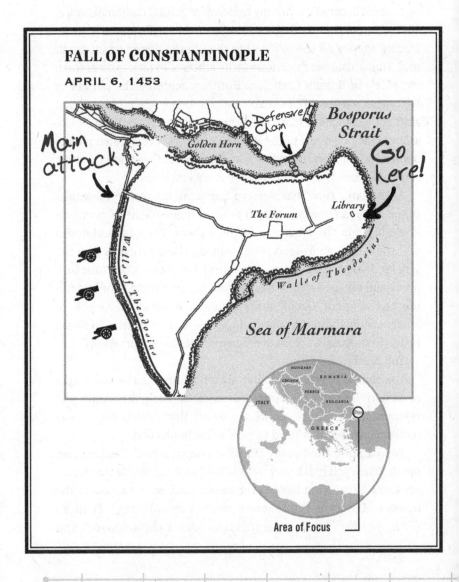

FALL OF CONSTANTINOPLE

APRIL 6, 1453

Main attack

Defensive Chain

Bosporus Strait

Golden Horn

Go here!

Library

The Forum

Walls of Theodosius

Walls of Theodosius

Sea of Marmara

Area of Focus

* * *

In the early morning hours of May 29 the first wave of Ottoman soldiers crashes against the Constantinople defense, which means you'll need to leave the library and return to the wall to avoid a dangerous charge of dereliction.

Under the cover of dark, Mehmed sends out his first soldiers, the bashi-bazouk. These are his mercenaries: Slavs, Hungarians, Germans, Italians, and even a few Greeks, fighting for pay and the promise of booty. They probe the length of the walls, even testing some of the seawalls, but these forays are merely distractions. Their main aim, and what Mehmed believes is his best chance, are the weak walls above the Lycus River. For two hours they throw themselves against the wall—and for two hours they fail. They fight wildly and without discipline or organization. When they finally draw back, they leave behind thousands.

Mehmed is undeterred. The bashi-bazouk were his weakest soldiers, and his most expendable. Their goal was merely to tire. Before the sun even rises, Mehmed sends his second wave: the Anatolians. The Anatolians are devout Muslims, with better weaponry, better training, and motivated by far more than money. Unlike the mercenaries, they maintain their organization, successfully climb the walls with their ladders and grappling hooks, and bring the fight to the top. You may have to resort to hand-to-hand weaponry, including the dangerous blast of a culverin, to save yourself.

In the midst of this second wave, a cannonball smashes a hole in the outer wall, and the Anatolians rush through the gap. It may feel as if the end is near, but again the Byzantine defenders not only fight off the Anatolians on the parapets, they surround and repel the attackers. They beat back the Anatolians, push them through the hole in the wall, and you and the rest of the defenders can shore up the yawning gap.

By now, the fighting will have raged for four consecutive hours, and the Anatolians will have inflicted heavy casualties. You and the rest of the city's defense will be exhausted. Nevertheless, you will have again successfully repelled the Ottoman attack. Twice the Ottomans will have charged, and twice retreated with far fewer than they came with. You might think that yet again another empire has fatally bashed itself against the insurmountable Theodosian Walls.

Then Mehmed sends in his third and final wave.

At 4 a.m., still hours before the sun rises on the gruesome scene, Mehmed's Janissary troops march toward the wall. The Janissaries are the finest soldiers in the Ottoman army, the most disciplined and best trained. They are Mehmed's last hope. For a third time the Ottomans climb the walls on ladder and rope and fight along the parapets.

Reload your culverin, because once again the fighting will become personal, nasty, and face-to-face. But even though the Janissaries are more skilled, coordinated, and committed, the defense holds. Their attacks begin to falter, and as the sun rises you may again feel a glimmer of hope. Unfortunately, in the first light of day, a series of disasters will take place.

First, someone on the Byzantine defense has forgotten to seal a small port door in the wall called the Kerkoporta, which was used during the battle to sneak out and mount surprise attacks directly onto the enemy. Janissary soldiers notice the mistake and rush through, and at 6 a.m. a Janissary bullet strikes Giovanni Giustiniani, the commander of the defense. When Giovanni's men remove him from the battlefield, morale collapses. The defenders rush back into the city to try to save their lives and their families, and the tide of the battle turns decisively. The Janissaries open the Saint Romanus Gate from the inside and put Constantinople to the sack. Emperor Palaiologos is last seen charging into the oncoming wave. According to one account, blood flows in the Constantinople streets "like rainwater in the gutters after a sudden storm."

You need to move quickly.

If you're caught on the city streets, you'll be tortured, killed, or enslaved. Fortunately, the attackers will be momentarily motivated by treasure, and their greed provides two options for escape. The first leaves out of the city port, where a few ships successfully escape the unguarded mouth of the inlet. By midmorning, however, the Ottomans shut down the port for good. These early boats provide your best means for escape, but if you miss them, there is one final option: You can try to fight your way out.

In the three towers nearest the entrance to the Golden Horn, a remarkable group of tenacious Cretan warriors will refuse to run. They'll barricade themselves in the towers and use shield and spear to form a deadly blockade in the narrow stairways, clogging the corridors with the bodies of the Ottoman soldiers. The Cretans will successfully fend off the Ottoman attackers for more than eight hours, inflicting such heavy losses that the Ottomans will strike a truce. In exchange for their surrender, they'll allow the Cretans safe passage out of the city. Join up with these Cretan soldiers, pick up a shield and spear, and if you can survive the eight-hour battle—which by now will mean fifteen consecutive hours of hand-to-hand combat—then late in the afternoon you can board the last ships to leave the city.

The journey back to Europe may be long and arduous, and you'll arrive on a continent panicked by Constantinople's fall. But you'll also arrive to a culture with a burgeoning interest in science, the arts, philosophy, and an appreciation for the ancient books you (hopefully) carry. Just don't read them within earshot of the Vatican, and maybe don't read any more ads. Even if they are printed.

HOW TO SURVIVE

THE FIRST
CIRCUMNAVIGATION

Let's say you're an adventurous traveler with three years to spare. You're excited by new places, languages, and cultures. You want to explore, and you're not picky about your accommodations: You don't mind the refreshing splash of a rogue wave, the omnipresent stench of rotting meat and unwashed sailors, nor the putrid tang of urine-soaked hardtack.

So you travel back to Seville, Spain, on August 9, 1519, and you join Ferdinand Magellan's armada of fortune and discovery.

You'll embark on humanity's greatest documented voyage of exploration, sail off the edge of the known map, find the mythical strait through the American continent, complete the world's first circumnavigation, gain a day on the rest of the world, add 7,000 miles to its known circumference, actually accomplish what Christopher Columbus died thinking he had, and get rich all at the same time. You'll just have to survive first.

Not many did.

Of the 260 sailors and five ships that departed Seville on Magellan's great circumnavigation, only a single ship and eighteen sailors successfully returned. To earn a place alongside the world's first circumnavigators, you'll have to survive starvation, malnutrition, dehydration, desertion, treachery, shipwreck, sabotage, scurvy, sea battles, land battles, mutiny, and the most dangerous sea passage on earth.

Your first step: Pack appropriately.

As a common sailor, you'll be allotted a single trunk for your own personal cargo. Fill it wisely. For clothes, pack what the Spanish sailors wore: thin cheap linen shirts with a hood, a woolen pullover with rope cinched at the waist, and a large blue cape to wear in foul weather. Your pants should be light, baggy, and cut off just below the knees. Pack an empty jug to hold your allotment of wine, a deck of playing cards, and a few books to pass the time; bring plenty of knives to trade for fresh food in the Philippines and spices in Indonesia; and—*most important of all*—buy as many jars of the pear-like quince jam as you can. It's a little expensive, but it'll be worth it.

Arrive on the docks on the evening of August 9, look the part of a salty sailor, and you should land a job. The armada struggled to recruit sailors for reasons you'll soon experience. Magellan's recruiters trawled every bar and alley from Seville to Gibraltar to round up enough sailors willing to sign up for a two-year voyage to an undisclosed destination, so he could hardly be picky. Haul your trunk, pull up your pajama pants, don your bonete, and you should find a spot on board.

The crew Magellan cobbled together originated from across Europe. They spoke German, French, Catalan, Spanish, Italian, and Greek, among other tongues, so your language barrier needn't be one. Most have more experience than you, but there is one crew member who doesn't—and he might be the most important of them all. Antonio Pigafetta was a short-statured Italian who traveled Spain in want of adventure, and when he heard of Magellan's upcoming voyage he begged his way aboard by offering his services as the armada's diarist. Remarkably, and despite his inexperience, Pigafetta was one of the eighteen who successfully returned, and his detailed and at times eloquent account of the journey provided the primary source for the great voyage. Stick with him.

Tied to the Seville docks you'll find five tar-blackened ships readying for sail: the *San Antonio*, the *Concepción*, the *Victoria*, the *Santiago*, and the flagship *Trinidad*. Each is about the size of a midsized modern yacht, between 60 and 70 feet long and displacing between 80 and 120 tons. They're built in the Spanish "carrack" style, with shallow drafts to allow passage down the Guadalquivir River from Seville to the open sea: They have three masts, and a U-like design with a low middle but fore and aft decks that rise more than thirty feet above the waterline. The top-heavy design results in violent swings in even moderate seas but, unintuitively, decreases the likelihood of a capsize. Seasickness, however, will be a concern.

If you have a choice, board the armada's flagship *Trinidad*, which is under the direct stewardship of the captain-general himself, Ferdinand Magellan. This is important—though not because Magellan is a captain you'll enjoy working for. You almost certainly won't.

Magellan was a short, stocky, intense man with a jet-black beard and a cold, analytical demeanor that made him intensely disliked by both his subordinates and his king. His obsession for the glory of this voyage drove him into exile from his native Portugal, and he risked torture and death before the ships even left the docks. In other words, he will never turn these ships around. Not if it means his life, and certainly not if it means yours. That would seem to make him a poor choice for your captain—and when his co-captains learn of his appetite for risk, they will desire for a change in leadership. But even if he will gladly risk your life in pursuit of his strait, he is also one of the few with the skills to save it.

Born the son of a mayor in the town of Sabrosa, Magellan enlisted in the Portuguese navy just as it began to convert the great exploratory missions of legendary Portuguese captains like Bartolomeu Dias and Vasco da Gama into empirical power. At age twenty-four he sailed alongside 1,500 sailors and twenty ships in Portugal's first great armada to the east and was wounded in Portugal's great naval victory against 200 Indian ships at the Battle of Cannanore. Three years later he rounded the Cape of Good Hope again, this time on an exploratory mission to the Malaysian city of Malacca, where Magellan bought an enslaved man of mysterious origin who he baptized as "Enrique." Remember the name.

While in Malacca, Magellan also happened to save the life of a fellow Portuguese sailor named Francisco Serrão. Serrão would later be among the first Europeans to set foot on the so-called Spice Islands, or Moluccas (Indonesia's Maluku archipelago). He wrote to Magellan informing him of the riches growing from their soil and—most intriguingly—their location, which his letters revealed was so far to the east that Magellan believed he could reach them faster by sailing west from Portugal, rather than east, if he could find a passage through the Americas.

When Magellan returned to Portugal, he presented his plan to the Portuguese King Manuel I, but Manuel—sitting in perhaps the same seat that King João II had when he declined Christopher Columbus—refused. So, like Columbus, Magellan turned to Spain, not only risking treason, torture, and execution, but—by sailing with that country—also creating a mutinous cocktail before he even departed. Though he was "captain-general" of the armada, the captains of the four other ships were all Spaniards and were therefore both jealous and suspicious of their Portuguese commander.

Nevertheless, on the morning of August 10, 1519, you, the *Trinity*, and the rest of the "Armada de Moluccas" depart the docks in Seville, make your way down the Guadalquivir River, and into the Atlantic.

Six weeks later you stop at the island of Tenerife just long enough for two incredibly unfortunate events to take place. First, the vendors cheat you out of a life-threatening amount of food. And second, Magellan learns the Portuguese have dispatched warships to capture, jail, torture, and likely execute him. To escape, Magellan charts the course of a madman. He sails south down the stormy African coast rather than immediately across the Atlantic. But not wanting to tell his suspicious Spanish comrades that his already controversial presence has put them all in great peril, he neglects to inform them about the purpose of his dangerous course, which sparks the first attempted mutiny. It won't be the last.

High winds and huge waves lash at your helpless ships for sixty straight days. Pigafetta writes that during one particularly heavy storm, the sailors feel death is so certain they begin to weep. You may not be as concerned. As seasick as you are, you may wish for it. Yet death somehow never arrives, the seas finally calm, and the winds steady. You cross the Atlantic, sailing down the South American coast and past what is now Brazil, and arrive at the edge of the world known to Europeans on January 10, 1520.

There, at the Río de la Plata, Magellan begins his search for the mythical strait through the American continent. The yawning mouth of the Río de la Plata, which today separates Argentina and Uruguay, offers the first hope. For three days the armada sails up the wide river mouth, hoping to find the Pacific but instead discovering fresh water. It's the first of many false hopes.

As you continue south, Magellan slows his ships to ensure he doesn't sail past his strait. He sails only during the day and hugs the shoreline so tightly that on more than one occasion the boats beach themselves on shoals. He searches every bay, river, and gulf, looking for a passageway through the continent, but by doing so slows his progress and increases the danger. Summer transitions to fall as you sail into one of the stormiest regions on earth. By March 31, after battling increasingly frequent and violent storms, an especially harrowing gale convinces even Magellan that you cannot continue. But rather than turn around, Magellan anchors your armada in the protected but cold and desolate bay of San Julián, 400 miles from the southern tip of South America.

For six months you spend the cold winter with poor shelter and meager rations. Unsurprisingly, morale suffers and the mood turns mutinous.

On the night of Easter Sunday, Juan de Cartagena, the expedition's second-in-command, convinces Gaspar de Quesada and Luis de Mendoza, the Spanish captains of the *Concepción* and *Victoria*, to mutiny, using as his cause the dangerous route that Magellan took down the coast of Africa and the not-indefensible belief that his fanatical search will kill them all. When the captain of the *San Antonio*, Magellan's cousin Álvaro de Mezquita, refuses to join, they kill his second-in-command, put Mezquita in irons, and commandeer his ship.

At this point Magellan is outnumbered three ships to two. You may think it prudent to switch sides. Don't. Despite a disadvantage in ships, armaments, and men, Magellan still has two significant advantages: First, he is far more skilled and experienced than his mutinous captains. And second, mutineers were nearly always reluctant participants because the crown considered the crime categorically indefensible and punishable by torture and death. So whereas the mutinous sailors lack conviction, Magellan has the resolve of a captain committed to death before he will hand over command. When the mutineers offer to negotiate, Magellan strikes. He sends over two boats of "negotiators" to

Mendoza. They cut his throat and easily reconvert the ambiguously mutinous crew.

The remaining ships surrender without a shot fired. Magellan is unforgiving of the mutiny's leadership. He quarters and displays Mendoza's mangled body, executes Quesada, and tortures the expedition's chief pilot and suspected conspirator Andrés de San Martín. Rather than execute the politically connected Juan de Cartagena and his assisting priest, Magellan maroons them on the Patagonian coast. Neither was ever heard from again. You, as a loyal Magellanite (never a doubt!), should live on.

With the mutiny quelled, Magellan spends the rest of the winter in San Julián organizing numerous scouting missions to hunt for the strait he believes is close. Avoid every one of them. They all end as starving failures, but a particularly consequential one occurs when the *Santiago* sails on a search mission south. After only a few miles, giant waves smash the ship on the rocks. The crew manages to leap ashore before waves splinter the boat but is left stranded twelve miles from the rest of the rest of the armada, with the three-mile-wide Santa Cruz river blocking their path back. They spend a month shivering and surviving on raw shellfish while two of their strongest navigate the treacherous river on a raft constructed from the splinters of their ship, then trek another eleven days with almost no food or water to reach Magellan and form a rescue party. Somehow, none of the crew died after their monthlong ordeal.

Finally, on October 18, 1520, the weather breaks and the now four-ship armada departs south. Three days later, on October 21, you spot a gap in the shoreline. At first, it may appear like the countless bays and river mouths you've seen and searched before. The entrance spans just a mile and a half, narrower than some of the rivers you've already searched. But unlike the brackish rivers, crystal-blue water pours from the gap while whale bones litter the long beach at its entrance—a sure sign you've found a migratory route. According to Pigafetta, Magellan doesn't doubt for a moment what he's found. Seven years since first planning his voyage, he has discovered his strait.

As you enter the inlet between the mainland of South America and the island of Tierra del Fuego, you'll see ice sheets that spill down from the Patagonian highlands and tower more than 500 feet above the water's edge. To your south, distant fires, perhaps lit by humans, burn so frequently they cast an eerie orange glow across the island's horizon. But elation at your discovery and awe at its beauty may transition to fear when you first experience the risks. Inside the protected channel, you're safe from large open-ocean swells, but the strait has its own peculiar dangers. Super-winds called williwaws flow down from the top of the Andes mountains into the sea, blasting through the narrow channels and threatening to push your boats into the rocks. Meanwhile, glaciers calve off in shipwrecking chunks with disturbing regularity, and twenty-foot tidal swings render almost every anchorage a potentially ship-tearing berth. Of all these challenges, though, none pose as great a threat as navigation itself. Rather than cut a direct route to the Pacific, the strait zigzags for more than 300 miles of false paths, dead ends, islands, and narrow channels. It resembles a maze more than a shipping passage. At every turn Magellan has to dispatch scouting ships and send sailors to the top of mountains to find the way forward. Years from now, Magellan's successful navigation of the strait and its spiderweb-like configuration of false passageways, bays, inlets, glaciers, islands, and powerful winds will be regarded as perhaps the single greatest navigational feat of the Age of Sail. But for now, it's frustrating, cold, and dangerous.

As you continue, the strait's terrifying gusts convince some of the crew that without retreat, death is certain within this icy labyrinth at the end of the world. Yet despite their protestations,

STRAIT OF MAGELLAN

OCTOBER 21, 1520

your captain refuses to abandon his quest. During one scouting mission, a storm nearly sinks the *San Antonio*, and the will of the ship's pilot and second-in-command, Estêvão Gomes, finally breaks. Having already beseeched Magellan to return to Spain, Gomes takes the arrival of the storm as an opportunity to do so himself. He organizes a mutiny against its captain Mezquita, locks him below deck, then slips past the rest of the armada and sails for home.

When the *San Antonio* fails to return, Magellan surmises what has occurred and realizes it will make for an awkward return to

Spain. In order to avoid a mutineer's execution upon their return, Gomes and the crew of the *San Antonio* will have to disparage Magellan and the rest of the armada in the harshest terms. Don't expect songs and celebration when you arrive back in Seville.

But that's a problem years in the making. For now, the ship's mutiny poses a more pressing concern. The *San Antonio* was the armada's largest ship. It held the lion's share of your dwindling provisions, and its desertion turns an unstable food situation desperate. The crew begs Magellan to sail for Spain to resupply and return. Magellan sails onward.

On November 28, 1520, after thirty-seven days spent navigating the strait, and with only three ships of the original five remaining, you finally reach the Pacific Ocean.

According to Europe's best maps and thus Magellan's sincerest beliefs, the Pacific Ocean is but a narrow strait. He believes the crossing is, at most, a few hundred miles. Had he known its true girth, even Magellan would have surely turned back.

Magellan's maps were off by almost 7,000 miles. Expecting the quick riches and salvation of the Spice Islands at any moment, the armada instead sails into the world's largest body of water. As the days stretch into weeks, and the weeks into months, the meat rots and the hardtack goes soft. Even the water turns foul. You'll eat and drink it anyway.

"We ate biscuit which was no longer biscuit, but powder of biscuits swarming with worms, for they had eaten the good. It stank strongly of the urine of rats. We drank yellow water that had been putrid for many days," wrote Pigafetta. Oxhides and sawdust become a staple, rats a delicacy. But even as your stores of food almost completely deplete, it isn't the lack of food that poses the danger. It's the kind of food.

Beginning in the second month of your journey across the Pacific, you'll watch as the sailors around you sicken and die from a disease new to Europeans known as scurvy. The symptoms begin in the gums, which first swell and squish, then become splotchy, blacken, and rot before finally losing their grip on the teeth, which begin to fall. Painful ulcers develop in the legs and arms that soon become gangrenous and blacken. After the excruciating final stages of scurvy, "death arrives as a merciful release," the explorer Robert Falcon Scott wrote, usually in the form of a burst blood vessel in the brain or heart.

Because the theory of disease transmission in this era centered on "bad air" or "miasmas," the doctors and captains aboard will probably tell you something inherent to sea air causes this terrible affliction. The dampness of the breeze, perhaps, or the stench of the hold. But while the latter is so foul the theory may seem plausible, scurvy instead results from a lack of vitamin C, which the body requires to synthesize collagen.

Collagen is the body's binding agent. It ties muscle, skin, and tissue together. The word itself originates from the Greek word for "glue." Without collagen, the body simply falls apart.

Most animals, including the rats in the cargo hold, can synthesize their own vitamin C (so eat rats if your gums begin to squish). Humans, however, must ingest it or die. Fortunately, we don't need much. A healthy person can survive six months without any vitamin C, and a diet with nearly any fresh food provides enough. As a result, scurvy requires a diet of purely preserved foods for more than six months, which is such an unusual circumstance that, outside of a few ancient and particularly destitute military campaigns, scurvy didn't arise until the long voyages in the Age of Sail.

The first documented cases occurred on Vasco da Gama's expeditions to India in 1498, when many of the sailors sickened, and thirty died. Oddly, da Gama's records suggest his sailors learned fresh citrus seemed to cure the disease. On the return journey, the sick requested oranges. Thus, da Gama's trip would seem to represent both the beginning and the end for the terrible disease. It wasn't. Over the next 400 years, more than 2 million sailors died of scurvy. The deficiency killed more sailors than shipwrecks, war, and all other diseases combined. On long voyages, captains expected it to kill half their sailors. How this carnage occurred despite an astonishingly simple, cheap, and abundant cure that produced near-immediate results with numerous anecdotal reports of its efficacy, stemmed from two central problems: First, even though the cure is simple, the mechanism behind its action is both complex and at the time was a complete mystery. The entire science of nutrition remained a black box during the Age of Sail, and with no understanding of vitamins, the peculiarities of scurvy's cure were difficult to correctly interpret. Despite its abundancy, many preservation methods destroy vitamin C, including heat. As a result, doctors would observe scurvy-sickened sailors drink pasteurized citrus juice, die, and thus defensibly dismiss the remedy as another superstition of the sea.

Second, doctors struggled to recommend a medication without understanding the process behind its effect. Even the most brilliant doctors of the era would observe unambiguous proof of the cure, but then wouldn't prescribe it because doing so would admit their ignorance of the disease's cause. The most notable example of this occurred in 1747, when the British naval surgeon James Lind conducted what is regarded as the first controlled drug trial in medical history. While aboard the scurvy-riddled HMS *Salisbury*, Lind identified twelve sickened sailors "who were as similar as I could make them," he later wrote, separated them into pairs, and treated them each with a different rumored cure. To one pair he prescribed vinegar, to another a liter of seawater—and to a third he administered a daily orange and lime.

The results proved as miraculous as they were dispositive. By the sixth day, the two sailors eating citrus had recovered to such a degree that they provided aid to the sickest—presumably the ones forcing down seawater.

And yet Lind fell into the same trap as the doctors before him. He wrote a 450-page treatise on his study and spent the majority of those pages positing ridiculous hypotheses on scurvy's cause, finally deciding upon a theory relating to a blockage of perspiration caused by the dampness at sea. Lind's brilliantly designed study should have saved millions, and yet he buried the lede in 450 pages of absurdity, then compounded his mistake by suggesting sailors boil the juice to preserve it without having tried that ill-advised technique himself. Predictably, his study, despite the genius of its design, had no effect.

It took another forty years and a doctor with a keen sense of observation, a bureaucrat's fastidiousness for detail, and the humility to admit what he didn't know to finally bring an end to the disease's terrible toll.

Gilbert Blane was the fourth son of a wealthy merchant. Educated in medicine in Scotland, he moved to London as a young doctor, where he distinguished himself despite a demeanor so icy his medical students nicknamed him "Chilblain"* and a face so scowled one contemporary newspaper described him as having a "deathlike expression of countenance." Yet in 1781 the admiral George Brydges Rodney appointed him physician of the fleet for his twenty-ship armada to the West Indies.

As chief physician, Blane weaponized his obsession for detail by requiring the surgeons on all twenty ships to file daily reports on every sick sailor in their charge. These reports reveal a striking truth about the Royal Navy: They indeed faced a ruthless enemy on the high seas, but it was hardly the Spanish Armada. After two years at sea and a fight in the "moonlight battle," Rodney's fleet

---

*"Chilblain" is the medical term for a small itchy red patch that can appear on cold skin.

suffered 715 casualties—yet only 8 percent of those deaths occurred in combat. The rest had succumbed to disease. Toward the end of the voyage, the fleet lost twenty sailors a month to scurvy alone. Yet from Blane's detailed reports, he could see every ship in the armada suffered, with the notable exception of the single ship that had happened to resupply on oranges midvoyage.

Blane was already familiar with Lind's experiment, he wrote in his book *Observations on the Diseases of Seamen,* and with that experiment plus his own observations he began treating his sailors with citrus. He ordered citrus treated with alcohol as a preservative instead of heat, which, as he noted, seemed to ruin the effect. Deaths by scurvy fell to zero. Though the Royal Navy initially ignored Blane's calls to issue limes navy-wide, in 1795 he was appointed Commissioner of the Sick and Hurt for the entire Royal Navy and instituted a ration of citrus to all ships. By 1825, his lime-alcohol cocktail had effectively eradicated the disease.*

Remarkably, Blane avoided the pratfall of theorizing why his treatment worked, merely writing, "In what manner they [fresh foods] produce their effect, I am at a loss to determine, never having been able to satisfy my mind with any theory concerning the nature and cure of this disease, nor hardly indeed of any other." He did, however, allow himself to wonder if scurvy didn't derive from what he called "a deficiency of wholesome ailment"—which

---

*However, in a demonstration of the difficulty of treating scurvy before the discovery of vitamins, a century later the disease returned when doctors again doubted the efficacy of citrus—though not without reason. By the nineteenth century the world's navies had transitioned to such poorly preserved citrus that the fruit no longer retained vitamin C, yet steamships and faster transit times obscured this dangerous development. When the early Antarctic explorers like Robert Falcon Scott began to again live for months on preserved food and suffer from scurvy despite their citrus rations, they discarded the old theory in favor of new ones. Babies also began to sicken and die as preserved baby food replaced mother's milk. The disease wasn't truly eliminated until Albert Szent-Györgyi definitively identified vitamin C and its role in the body.

might be the earliest written postulation for the existence of something a century later would be called "vitamins."

As you depart the strait and enter the great Pacific Ocean, you need one vitamin in particular. During the long hibernation in Patagonia, fresh seal meat provided enough vitamin C to keep you alive. But when the weeks in the Pacific stretch into months and your gums begin to squish, you need to dig into the bottom of your trunk, find the pear-like quince jam you purchased in Seville, and spread it liberally onto your hardtack. It has just enough vitamin C to save your life.

It so happened that on Magellan's voyage the ship's officers were issued quince while the regular seamen were not. This had nothing to do with scurvy. The sugar was the perk of being an officer, not the as yet unknown vitamin C. But the small globs of jam were enough to save the officers while the sailors began to die daily during the ninety-eight-day crossing.

Early on the morning of March 6, 1521, after sailing 7,000 miles and completing the longest uninterrupted sea voyage ever recorded up to that time, you'll hear "Tierra!" shouted from the ship's lookout and soon watch as the islands of Rota and then Guam rise up from below the horizon. As you sail into the bay of Guam, hundreds of Chamorro people greet you on small proa boats stuffed with lifesaving fruits and fish.

At first, relations between the armada and the local people of the South Pacific progress cordially. You gladly trade your European-made goods for much-needed food. But following a pattern that will repeat itself in months ahead, the relationship soon breaks down thanks to misunderstandings and an increasingly imperialistic Magellan, who develops an increasing zeal to convert the local tribes you encounter to Christianity and the rule of Spain.

Most of those you encounter do "convert" and swear allegiance to King Carlos I of Spain—presumably because neither act has any practical effect other than to pacify Magellan. But some refuse. And to those, Magellan resorts to violence. He burns homes and kills the local people. Initially, he goes largely unopposed, increasing his false sense of military imperiousness.

On March 28, you arrive in the Philippine island of Mazaua. The locals greet the ship and, as on Guam, shout greetings at the crew. Except, unlike at Guam, this time someone understands them. To the shock of everyone aboard, Enrique—the enslaved man who Magellan had bought eight years before in Malacca—speaks back. The implications could not be more profound. It had been many years since slave traders ripped Enrique from his home and sold him to Magellan in Malacca. Since then, he had traveled from Malaysia to India, Africa, Portugal, Brazil, Patagonia, across the Pacific, and now he had returned home. On March 28, 1521, the enslaved man known only as "Enrique" becomes the first human to ever circumnavigate the globe.

On April 7, you'll arrive on the Philippine island of Cebu, where Magellan makes fast allies with the local chief Humabon. Humabon happily converts to Christianity and swears allegiance to King Carlos, but when he asks the chiefs of the neighboring islands to do the same, his rival Lapu-Lapu, chief of the nearby island Mactan, refuses. Magellan sees the refusal as another opportunity for glory. On the morning of April 27, 1521, despite the protestations of his officers, Magellan and sixty sailors set off in skiffs to attack Mactan.

Do not join them.

When Magellan and his soldiers disembark their longboats and wade through the shallow waters toward the island, 1,500 Mactanese warriors greet them on the beach. The warriors wield two-handed machete swords called kampilans, launch bamboo spears, and fire poison arrows. The Spanish armor protects their heads and torsos, but leaves their legs exposed. As they slowly make their way toward the beach, the poison begins to take its effect. The sailors begin to fall, including Magellan's own stepson. Shortly after arriving on the beach, Magellan orders a retreat back to the boats. But for him it's too late. With a poisoned arrow already lodged in his thigh and a bamboo spear in his shoulder, he falters. The Mactan warriors, recognizing their enemy, focus their assault.

From the decks of the *Trinidad* and far out of range, you'll watch the Portuguese navigator's attempt to encircle the world end in the shallow waters of that Philippine island. Pigafetta, who joined the assault yet managed to escape with a few others, wrote of Magellan's final moments: "Then the Indians threw themselves upon him, with spears and scimitars and every weapon they had, and ran him through—our mirror, our light, our comforter, our true guide—until they killed him."

The armada elects the Spaniard Juan Serrano as the new captain. His first decision is to ignore Magellan's will, which calls for Enrique to be freed and paid. This is a grave mistake—and not just for reasons of morality.

Enrique is, to put it mildly, displeased. According to Pigafetta, he speaks with Humabon and then informs you, the crew, and the captain that Humabon has cordially invited you all to a lavish dinner before the ships depart.

Skip it. Claim a stomachache, say you've already eaten, graciously give up your seat, or just hide—because Enrique is about to have his revenge.

Thirty sailors accept the invitation, a group that comprises a quarter of the remaining crew, Captain Serrano, and most of the senior officers. Halfway through the meal, you'll watch from the boat as Humabon's soldiers slaughter every last one except, perhaps, for the world's first circumnavigator. He's never heard from again.

That night you finally depart the Philippine archipelago with only 115 of the original 260 sailors.* So few sailors remain that you burn the *Concepción* for want of crew. With Magellan gone, you abandon religious conversions and rededicate yourselves to finding the Moluccas. But lacking the navigational genius of Magellan along with most of the senior officers, you spend months bouncing from island to island in the South Pacific. This is a long, listless period alternately spent kidnapping local guides, beaching yourselves on reefs, and spending more months repairing the damage.

Finally, on November 8, 1521, more than twenty-seven months after leaving Seville, you enter the bay of the Spice Island Tidore.

As real as the dangers have been on this journey, so are the riches. Clove spices worth more in Europe than their weight in gold fall from the trees. Here, they're mostly worthless. The locals happily trade them for the knives and mirrors you've brought from Seville. Trade for a few sacks full and you can retire rich. Over the next six weeks, you load almost 3,000 pounds of cloves—worth more than $6 million in today's money—into your two vessels.

But before you depart, you need to switch ships. Just as the armada prepares to leave, you discover a disastrous leak in the *Trinidad* that requires months of repair. The delay would prevent you from riding the trade winds west, so you decide to split. The *Victoria* immediately departs west for Spain, while the *Trinidad* will finish its repairs and then ride the trade winds east across the Pacific to Panama, where mules will carry the spices across the isthmus, load them onto a ship, and sail them home.

Most of the crew prefers to sail on the *Trinidad*, believing that those attempting the Indian Ocean would either starve to death

---

*On May 5, the *San Antonio* arrived back in Seville. To avoid charges of mutiny, the sailors call you, Magellan, and the rest of the armada traitors. This will create some awkwardness when you return to Spain.

or wreck in the dangerous waters beneath the Cape of Good Hope. They're wrong. The *Victoria*'s journey will indeed be hellish, but you need to join it, because the *Trinidad*'s is worse. It will become hopelessly lost in the Pacific, suffer horrific bouts of scurvy, return to the Philippines, and be captured by the Portuguese, who execute the captain for sailing in "Portuguese waters" and sentence the crew to hard labor.

For you, on your new home the *Victoria*, conditions will be an improvement to a beheading, but only slightly. After struggling west through the expanse of the Indian Ocean, you'll run into an elemental wall beneath the Cape of Good Hope. Currents, waves, and winds blast beneath the African continent, pinning your ship in perpetual storm along the deadliest stretch of sea on earth. Again and again you try to round the cape only to be beaten back. The leaks in the ship worsen and the supplies dwindle to the point that some want to abandon the attempt entirely and turn themselves in to the Portuguese-controlled island of Madagascar, where you would surely be imprisoned and possibly executed. But these men are overruled. After nine straight weeks of failed attempts, the winds briefly lighten, the waves lessen, the currents abate, and on May 22, 1522, you slip around the southernmost point on the African continent.

Celebrate with some quince, because it's been months since you have eaten fresh food, and once again scurvy strikes. Over the next six weeks, twenty-one sailors out of the remaining fifty-eight die for want of vitamin C.

On July 9, you reach the Portuguese-controlled Cape Verde islands off the coast of what is now Senegal. Desperate and unable to continue without fresh supplies, you risk the port and lie about your identity to acquire food. It works. At least initially.

But while in port, a most curious event occurs. You learn from the Portuguese at port the day is Thursday. This is perplexing. Pigafetta and the other diarists on board are convinced it is

Wednesday. As Pigafetta wrote, "It was a great cause of wondering to us, since with us it was only Wednesday. We could not persuade ourselves that we were mistaken; and I was more surprised than the others, since having always been in good health, I had every day, without intermission, written down the day that was current."

Astoundingly, there is no mistake. From your perspective, it is Wednesday. From the Europeans', it is Thursday. As the world's first circumnavigators, you've discovered the peculiar reward for circling the globe. By gaining a few minutes on the sun each day as you chased it west, you've gained a day on the world. More than two centuries later, the installation of the International Date Line in the Pacific will end the confusion. But for now, after 1,084 days on the water, one is missing. Pigafetta's discovery will later shock Europe, for none of its scholars had predicted this amazing consequence of circumnavigation.

Unfortunately, even this close to home, your suffering has not yet ended. As you prepare to leave Cape Verde, you send one last boat with thirteen sailors to gather supplies. Make sure you're not on it.

The Portuguese discover the deception and arrest the men onshore. You and the *Victoria* escape and begin the final push to Spain. Almost two months later, you and 18 of the original 260 sailors turn your tattered boat up the Guadalquivir River and tie up at the Seville docks almost exactly three years after you departed, on Saturday, September 10, 1522 . . . Or is it Sunday?

HOW TO SURVIVE
A VOYAGE WITH BLACKBEARD

Let's say you want to join up with a bold group of entrepreneurs pursuing a lucrative opportunity in international trade. You want to take an equal partnership alongside a skilled team of equally dedicated founders chasing life-changing payouts, and you don't mind a bit of adventure. Or a bit of risk. So you travel back to the city of Nassau on the Bahamian island of New Providence in the year 1717. It's the height of piracy's golden age, back when pirate crews operated out of their own capital city, stole some of the most lucrative treasures in the history of criminal enterprise with firepower rivaling that of the European navies, and grew so powerful that they brought Atlantic sea trade to a near standstill.

But you don't want to work with just any pirate captain. You want to sail with the best. You want to sail alongside the most famous and most feared pirate of all time. So you arrive in Nassau on September 29, 1717, to join up with a certain black-bearded, Bristol-born pirate named Edward Thatch just as he assumes command of the *Revenge* and sails out of Nassau port.

* * *

Over the next month, Thatch unleashes the most devastating pirate assault the British colonies have ever witnessed. In just two weeks he captures fifteen merchant ships as they approach ports in Delaware, Philadelphia, New York, and the Chesapeake. He plunders their cargo and recruits so many of their crewmen to turn pirate that he adds another ship to his pirate fleet. But those who don't turn to his side he sends on their way, because despite Thatch's bravado and fearsome reputation, he has a secret: He's unusually hospitable to those he captures.*

Over the fall of 1717, hijacked seafarers pour into the sea towns of Europe and the Americas telling tales of a tall, slim pirate with a long black beard, a bandolier of pistols, and a face obscured by fire (a result of fuses he lit and tucked under his cap). According to one account, "imagination cannot form an idea of a fury from hell to look more frightful." In just one month after assuming command, the pirate captain Edward Thatch has become the pirate legend Blackbeard.

Over the next fifteen months, Blackbeard will terrorize the shipping lanes of the Atlantic, the Gulf of Mexico, and the Caribbean. He will rob more than a hundred ships, siege the city of Charleston, and, at his height, command a pirate fleet so formidable that ships of the Royal Navy itself flee at mere rumors of his presence. Then, just over a year after taking command, he'll be killed in a bloody sea battle.

But you can survive. You can commit some of the most lucrative heists in criminal history and live to spend the riches. But before you survive the bloody sea battles, you'll need to learn how to survive the greatest threat of all: your fellow pirates. You'll need to learn the rules—because you're not joining an anarchic group of nihilists. This sophisticated criminal enterprise might seem like a

---

*Remarkably, over Thatch's entire career, there is not a single documented case of him ever having killed anyone until his final battle.

floating anarchy from the outside. But because these seemingly lawless rebels cannot count on the authorities to fairly adjudicate transgressions, they have to rely on their own codes, and their own punishments, to keep disagreements at bay and rule breakers in line. The result is that, like most organized crime syndicates, these supposed rebels operate under a far more prescriptive set of behavioral boundaries than the outside world's.

Unfortunately, the rules specific to Blackbeard's boats have never been found. But we do have at least some idea of what you can expect, because the rules to the contemporary pirate captain Bartholomew "Black Bart" Roberts's ship have survived. These rules are as follows:

Bedtime belowdeck is at 8 p.m. sharp. There shall be no noise belowdeck after that hour. No fighting on board. Any disagreements will be resolved on the beach with pistol and sword. No gambling, period. No desertion, and of course no stealing from the ship. There are no women allowed on board, either. Plus there's an oddly specific rule against disguising a women as a man on board, the punishment for which is the default: death, though how that is meted out varies. Walking the plank is a Hollywood invention, but marooning is not. If you sail with Blackbeard expecting an anything-goes, "it's a pirate's life for me" free-for-all, you'll waste away on a deserted island with a single pistol shot as your only salvation.

You also need to know how to speak like a pirate. English was the lingua franca among the multicultural crew, who originated from across Europe, Africa, and the Caribbean. The majority, though, were born in England or its colonies. Surprisingly, Hollywood's pirate accent ("Arrrrr matey," etc.) is an exaggerated approximation of the truth. It's a form of the Cornwall accent, which is the coastal county on England's southwestern tip where many pirates were born. So drop your *h*'s and roll your *r*'s. Fortunately, even if your fake Cornish accent turns a few heads, because piracy is an extraordinarily diverse enterprise, your awkward *r*'s may not get you killed as quickly as you might think.

The same can sadly not be said for the viruses and bacteria you'll find aboard. You're not only sharing tight quarters with hundreds of unwashed sea dogs, you're eating rotting food, drinking contaminated water, and traveling to foreign lands rife with foreign ailments. It would be difficult to construct an unhealthier environment than the hull of a pirate ship. Here, disease will kill you as quickly as any cannonball. Pirate ships typically carried doctors, but if you should sicken, don't see one. At best, their medical care will be ineffective. At worst, you might receive something like the urethral injection of mercury that divers discovered on Blackbeard's wrecked *Queen Anne's Revenge*, which pirates used to treat syphilis. Decline that prescription. Try to eat fresh food, particularly if it's meat, and avoid water entirely. Drink the grog instead. It's a rum-water mixture of various dilutions as essential as sails to eighteenth-century ships. If you can follow the rules and dodge dysentery and disease, you should at least survive the first few months, because the first merchant vessels that Blackbeard attacked were no match for his armada.

After a month spent terrorizing the North American coast, Blackbeard departed the North Atlantic's rough winter seas for the calmer Caribbean. He patrolled the narrow shipping lanes of the Middle Passage, hunting for ships carrying enslaved Africans to the Americas. Pirates prized these infamous "slavers" not for their cargo but for the ships themselves. Unlike the open holds of their merchant vessel ships, a slave ship's multidecked structure could house both large pirate crews and enough cannons to rival anything in the Royal Navy. On November 17, 1717, after only two days lying in wait, Blackbeard spotted the huge sails of the French slave ship *La Concorde* and maneuvered his fleet upwind of his prey.

In eighteenth-century sea battles, a ship holding the upwind position on its opponent—called "holding the weather gauge"—provided several decisive advantages.

First, ships running upwind heel from the sidewise pressure of the wind, while ships running downwind stay level. The difference mattered in an exchange of cannon fire, because the aim of two-ton guns could not be adjusted quickly or easily. In an exchange of broadsides, the ship holding the weather gauge fired directly into the opponent while their enemy's cannonballs sailed overhead.

Second, while even modern sailboats cannot sail directly into the wind, warships in piracy's golden age couldn't move into the entire third of the upwind sky. As a result, a ship upwind of its opponent would have almost complete freedom of movement—while its opponent's would be pinned and predictable. This freedom allowed the upwind ship to perform a particularly devastating maneuver that naval strategists call "crossing the T," wherein the attacking ship cut across the path of its oncoming enemy. Because seventeenth-century warships had few or no cannon in the front or rear, the passing ship could unleash a full broadside without risk of return fire. A particularly skilled captain such as Blackbeard would veer within feet of his downwind opponent and fire cannonballs down the entire length of the ship.

Yet for pirates like Blackbeard, a broadside was a method of last resort. Broadsides risked sinking or damaging treasure. Instead, a pirate's preference was to engage the enemy in hand-to-hand combat, where sheer numbers gave them an overwhelming advantage. Blackbeard's ship carried as many as 300 sailors, while merchant vessels rarely held more than a few dozen. Using hooks, ropes, and ladders, pirates could lash the two boats together and swarm their victim in an overwhelming assault.

Of course, if a good pirate won sea battles, a great pirate avoided them entirely. Battles risked injury, death, damage to boats, or, worst of all, the treasure itself. So a great pirate cultivated an aura of bloodthirsty craziness, but combined it with a

reputation for mercy if the enemy surrendered. To help coax surrender, pirates signaled their bloody intentions with gruesome
flags of blood, skull, and bone. They gathered on deck, waved
their swords and guns, yelled threats, even wafted smoke
about their faces—anything to convey their seriousness to do
battle so that they wouldn't have to. Usually, it worked. Faced
with the overwhelming force of a pirate crew while protecting
cargo that was not their own, most merchant ships tried to flee,
but when cornered, few fought.

On November 17, the captain of *La Concorde* tries to escape,
but when it becomes clear he will be overtaken, he turns his vessel into the wind and raises a white flag. True to his reputation,
Blackbeard takes the ship but gives the crew of *La Concorde* one
of your smaller sloops (which they rename "*Bad Encounter*") and
sends them on their way.

Meanwhile, Blackbeard refits *La Concorde* with forty cannons,
crews it with 300 pirates, and renames it *Queen Anne's Revenge.**
With *QAR* as his flagship, Blackbeard not only commands one of
the most fearsome fleets in the Americas, he establishes one of the
most powerful criminal operations in world history.

Piracy has plagued the open seas for as long as ships have tra-
versed them, but the rise of its golden age began when an English
naval policy that leaned heavily upon military contractors back-
fired spectacularly. When war broke out against Spain in 1654,
England outsourced its military efforts by encouraging private

---

*They chose this name for political reasons. Most pirates were so-called Jaco-
bites who believed that, after Queen Anne's death, her house, the House of
Stuart, was the rightful ruler of England and thus supported her half brother
James's claim to the throne. But because James was a Catholic and Catholics
had been excluded by an act of Parliament, Anne's second cousin George I,
House of Hanover, ruled instead.

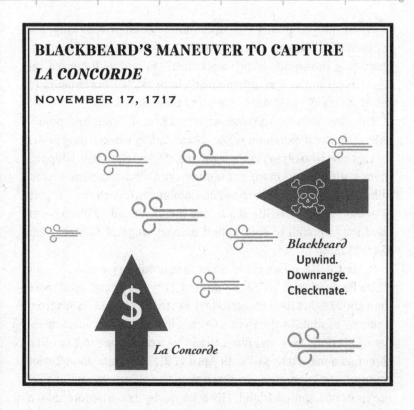

BLACKBEARD'S MANEUVER TO CAPTURE *LA CONCORDE*

NOVEMBER 17, 1717

Blackbeard
Upwind.
Downrange.
Checkmate.

La Concorde

citizens to legally pirate Spanish merchant ships. Under letters of marque, these legal pirates—called privateers—could lawfully keep a share of what they stole.

Business was good.

In 1671 the privateer Captain Henry Morgan and his fleet of thirty-seven ships and 2,000 privateers sacked the Spanish city of Panama and stole hundreds of thousands of pesos. King Charles II rewarded his efforts with the governorship of Jamaica. During the War of the Spanish Succession from 1701 to 1714, England expanded its usage of privateers, legalizing at least 1,400 ships to attack Spanish ships across the globe.

When the war finally ended, England halted privateering, but rediscovered the cost of outsourcing military efforts. After encouraging thousands of private citizens to pursue lucrative careers in piracy, the country asked these skilled buccaneers to return to poorly paid ones. Not all of them did.

The alternative for privateers was a brutal, brief, and poorly paid career as a merchant sailor. These sailors worked long hours for captains who often cut their rations, docked their pay, whipped them with the infamous cat-o'-nine-tails, and sometimes even killed them without repercussion. Combine this with the dangers of disease inherent in life at sea, and merchant sailors often never lived long enough to spend their meager wage of £25 per year ($4,000 today).

In contrast, a pirate could amass extraordinary wealth.

On September 7, 1695, the pirate Henry Every captured more than £600,000 ($100 million today) worth of gold and jewels from a convoy of ships in the Indian Ocean. In a single day, each member of his crew received more than they could hope to earn in a career as a merchant sailor. In April 1721, the pirate John Taylor captured the Portuguese treasure ship *Nossa Senhora do Cabo* off the coast of Reunion Island. His crew made off with more than a million pounds sterling—the equivalent of $160 million today. Each pirate on Taylor's ships took home approximately £4,000— more than a $500,000 today. And when a storm sank the pirate captain Sam Bellamy's *Whydah* off Cape Cod, it went down with more than four tons of gold and silver.

But gold wasn't the only reason for a sailor to choose piracy. Almost every facet of life aboard a pirate ship was more comfortable, and more equitable, than serving aboard a merchant vessel. Whereas merchant seamen often suffered under tyrannical captains, pirate ships operated as surprisingly democratic and even progressive institutions.

Almost a century before the French stormed the Bastille, pirate crews voted on their captains and placed a series of checks and balances on their power. Pirates elected a quartermaster to make all decisions regarding rations and punishments, and they voted on both where to sail and who to attack. Only during battle, which required snap decisions, could a captain rule unilaterally. Pirate captains slept in the same circumstances as the crew and received only a double share of the loot. When I asked Marcus Rediker, professor of Atlantic history at the University of Pittsburgh and author of *Villains of all Nations*, why these groups of cutthroats established proto-democracies, he tells me it was in part a response to horrific abuses of their previous lives. "The democratic nature of the pirate way of life was formed as a reaction against the top-down, violent, authoritarian nature of rule on naval and merchant ships," he explains. Many pirates were former merchant sailors who had mutinied against their authoritative, abusive, and violent captains. They had no interest in exchanging one tyrant for another. Instead, they turned pirate in large part because they believed in what Rediker writes was "a sailor's oppositional culture: equality, collectivism, and anti-authoritarianism." According to Rediker, these same values, which had animated their mutinies, guided the development of their floating societies.

But there may be an additional explanation for piracy's curiously democratic governing structure, according to George Mason University behavioral economist Peter Leeson: greed. According to Leeson, merchant vessels were particularly tyrannical because they suffered from the common business conundrum known as the "principal-agent problem," where those who do the work don't profit while those who profit don't do the work. Shipping merchants solved this problem by hiring tyrannical captains and including them in a share of the profit. These captains then had an incentive to both keep costs down and keep these otherwise poorly incentivized sailors working, which they did with a liberal use of corporal punishment.

But pirate ships were employee owned and operated. They didn't suffer from the principal-agent problem. They did the work and shared in the profits; thus they were already incentivized and had no use for tyrannical hierarchies. Like equal partners in a law firm, the pirate ship was a joint-venture agreement between all parties who all shared in the proceeds and all had an equal say in the direction of the operation—like a cross between a drug cartel and Goldman Sachs.

And yet curiously, unlike a drug cartel, piracy didn't devolve into a violent, highly hierarchical structure. When I ask Leeson why, he explains it's the result of the different start-up costs of each criminal business. A criminal enterprise that is cheap and easy to start—like drug dealing or the mafia's protection rackets—would, in a free market, face extremely stiff competition. If any bully with a gun is a potential competitor, start-up goons will undercut the market until no profit remains. The only way these criminal rackets can stay in business is to create illegal monopolies with violently enforced collusion agreements.

Piracy, however, required enormous start-up costs. A successful pirate needed a large ship, hundreds of pirates, guns, and food for the crew. These costs kept the business relatively uncompetitive, which negated the need to remove competitors with violence. In this case market forces, rather than morality, dictated moral choices. They also seem to have promoted a far more progressive racial composition than many of the era's other businesses.

Black pirates comprised around a third of all scallywags, and most received the same compensation and voting rights as white pirates. One of Blackbeard's closest lieutenants was a legendarily burly former African chieftain named Caesar. This is not to suggest that pirates were abolitionists—in fact, they certainly weren't. Many pirates had previously enslaved people, worked on slave ships, and allowed the captains of the slave ships they hijacked to continue on to their ports with enslaved people still on board. Nevertheless, witness testimony from prisoners on pirate ships suggests at least some or perhaps most Black pirates lived as free men with equal voting rights aboard pirate ships.

This, too, can probably be explained by a pirate's financial incentives rather than moral scruples. With 300 men on a ship that could be run by a dozen, there wasn't much need for manual labor and thus little incentive to enslave. On top of that, anyone working against their will represented a flight risk who might testify against the pirates in court. So, despite what we can only assume were a pirate's evil intentions, neither enslavement nor conscription made any rational sense. Unlike the Royal Navy, which employed "press-gangs" to roam the streets of London with clubs and handcuffs, beating, cuffing, and "pressing" any poor devil who looked like sailor material into naval service, pirates rarely conscripted, and only did so when the sailor possessed a rare and critical skill, such as doctors or gunsmiths.

You are not among men of great morality. But you are among a crew whose past, greed, and aversion to risk dictate a surprisingly progressive code of conduct—perhaps in spite of their best intentions.

On June 10, 1718, near the peak of Blackbeard's power and just after you siege the entire city of Charleston, South Carolina, *Queen Anne's Revenge* runs aground off the coast of North Carolina and the crew scatters. Blackbeard takes a small group of loyalists to meet with the governor of North Carolina, where he graciously accepts the king's pardon—and then continues pirating and paying off the governor with his stolen loot. He makes his base off the

North Carolina coast on Ocracoke Island (under what he believes is the governor's protection) and patrols the shipping lanes west of Bermuda.

You need to take this opportunity to say your goodbyes and depart, because unlike in the early days of his piracy, the economies of the Americas have begun to change. No longer do these economic backwaters produce rounding errors for the great European powers. Instead, as the eighteenth century entered maturity, these once small economies began to drive obscene accumulations of wealth and power. And while this might seem to make piracy all the more lucrative, instead it doomed the entire profession. Piracy has always flourished when the cost of its existence is lower than the cost of eradicating it. And in the Atlantic, the emergence of a new means to farm an old crop had begun to change that calculation.

On May 14, 1625, John Powell captained the first English ship to disembark on the Caribbean island of Barbados. By then, European diseases and more than a hundred years of Spanish slave raiding had wiped out the native population, so when Powell arrived, the island was almost completely uninhabited. English settlers established tobacco plantations and worked them with indentured English labor. But Barbados's small farms could hardly compete with the enormous tobacco fields in what is now the southern United States. As a result, its farms were only mildly profitable and its land cheap. In 1640, a farmer could purchase 500 acres of Barbados farmland for only 400 English pounds. Then came sugar.

Human cultures have harvested sugarcane for at least 10,000 years, but the process required such a herculean amount of labor it remained a luxury good as late as the mid-seventeenth century. For cane to grow, a farmer must clear, dig, and hoe the land, place each cane in a deep hand-dug hole, then fertilize the fields with handfuls of stinking dung. Fertilizer supercharges the growth of the cane but also the weeds, which, along with the cane-eating rats, the farmer must exterminate regularly.

Finally, when the plant ripens in the spring, the farmer must chop the thick stalk at its base, juice it, and then immediately boil the liquid before it spoils. Because of spoilage, sugar plantations are both farm and factory. There is no time to ship the cane off site, and crops must be processed so quickly that during the monthslong harvest season production runs twenty-four hours a day.

In the seventeenth century, workers in these plantations had to cut, press, boil, process, and dry the cane while operating heavy, dangerous equipment for longs shifts in hellish heat. In other words, sugar was an extraordinarily labor intensive, inefficient, lethal, and thus expensive good to produce, which limited its market to the very, very rich. That changed when the price of labor became very, very cheap.

In 1645, approximately 11,000 white English farmers and some 6,000 enslaved people farmed tobacco on the economically struggling island of Barbados. But in the 1640s, Dutch traders from Brazil introduced sugarcane. This "white gold," powered by the enslaved people who produced it, transformed the island. The crop showered wealth on landholders. By 1660, Barbados produced more wealth than all of England's American colonies combined. In just ten years, the price of 500 acres on Barbados rose from £400 to £7,000. Meanwhile, the demand for labor became insatiable. In just fifteen years, the population of the island grew from 17,000 to 53,000 people—more than half of whom were enslaved African laborers. By 1667, Barbados's wealthiest landowners consolidated their holdings. Impoverished white descendants of the early indentured English laborers and prisoners fled—some to piracy but most to the mainland—so that, by 1770, 40,000 enslaved Africans labored on sugar plantations controlled by just 750 white English owners. Sugar became the most lucrative product crossing the Atlantic, and sugar plantations quickly dominated the Caribbean. By 1714, the larger island of Jamaica outproduced Barbados. That year also marked the end to the War of the Spanish Succession, the treaty of which allowed Britain to greatly expand the number of enslaved people it could ship from Africa to the Americas.

Piracy threatened this lucrative business.

During the height of their golden age, pirates so thoroughly ravaged the ships crossing the Atlantic that they nearly severed the sugar and slave trade entirely. Between 1720 and 1722, as piracy reached a crescendo, the number of enslaved Africans shipped across the Atlantic dropped by half. In 1721, the governor of Antigua wrote to King George I that if piracy wasn't eliminated, "all of the English plantations in America will be totally ruin'd in a very short time."

England responded with increasing urgency. In 1718, the Crown issued pardons to any pirate who ceased piracy. Many pirates—including Blackbeard—gladly accepted this pardon. And then continued pirating.

So in 1721 Parliament withdrew the carrot and offered the stick. It passed the Piracy Act, which sentenced pirate sympathizers or business partners to death by hanging, threatened to imprison any merchant sailor who declined to defend their ship, and declared that navy captains could no longer conveniently avoid confrontations with powerful pirate fleets.

Finally, in 1722, in response to increasing pressure from slave traders, the British Admiralty sent ships of war to the west coast of Africa, where the pirate captain Black Bart had captured more than 400 ships over the previous three years and nearly single-handedly severed the Middle Passage. On February 10, 1722, the armada snuck up on Black Bart as he anchored off Gabon on the west coast of Africa, blasted the pirate captain with a broadside, and unofficially ended piracy's golden age. By 1725, with piracy in the Atlantic essentially eradicated, the yearly number of enslaved Africans shipped across the Middle Passage had doubled to more than 47,000.

The rise of the slave trade and the increasingly obscene amount of wealth shipped across the Atlantic paradoxically spells the end for piracy's golden age, and that's when you need to depart Blackbeard's company. To safely continue piracy, you need to leave this part of the world. So in the summer of 1718, catch a ride to the pirate-controlled island of Madagascar and join up with the pirate Captain John Taylor. Help him prowl the wealth passing through the Indian Ocean and capture the *Nossa Senhora do Cabo*, the most valuable heist in pirate history. Collect your share of the $160 million of diamonds, gold, and jewels, and safely hide away on Madagascar or another Spanish-controlled isle. Plundering the *Nossa Senhora* isn't without risks. The Portuguese carry quite a grudge— but, like Taylor, you should be able to purchase a pardon from a sympathetic Spanish court. And it's a far better option than continuing to ply the American coast with Blackbeard, where business interests have compelled the authorities to act.

In the fall of 1718, the governor of Virginia ordered Royal Navy lieutenant Robert Maynard, sixty soldiers, and two sloops to capture or kill the bearded pirate operating with impunity off the coast of North Carolina. On the morning of November 22, 1718, Maynard and his sloops entered the Ocracoke Island harbor where Blackbeard and his skeleton crew of twenty men lay at anchor.

As the boats neared, Blackbeard recognized the attack. He ordered his men to cannon and tried to make his escape. He sailed for the mouth of the bay and the open sea, and as he passed

Maynard he "drank Damnation to me and my Men . . . saying he would neither give nor take Quarter," according to a letter Maynard later wrote.

Maynard may have had the advantage in numbers, but in order to traverse the shallow waters he attacked with light ships lacking cannon. The decision nearly cost him his life. When Maynard attempted to pull up alongside the pirates, Blackbeard blasted broadsides into the impotent sloops, filling their decks with bodies and blood, killing Maynard's second-in-command, and disabling one of his ships. The blasts would have saved the pirates, Maynard later wrote, were it not for a lucky musket shot that severed Blackbeard's gib and foresail, allowing Maynard to catch up to the escaping pirates. In the ensuing battle, Blackbeard fell to five pistol shots. The rest of his crew was either killed or captured and hung.

Fortunately, you will have already departed. You'll be retired and sipping a grog cocktail on a Madagascar beach, or maybe you'll have started a venture fund investing in other pirate entrepreneurs seeking lucrative opportunities in international trade. Call it Adventure Capital.

HOW TO SURVIVE

THE DONNER PARTY

L et's say you want to strike it rich, but you've traveled back to 1846 and you're somewhere in the Midwest pulling potatoes out of the ground. You're tired of pulling potatoes. You want to pull gold. You want to try your luck and seek the fortunes buried in the foothills of the Sierra Nevada.* So you hitch up your Conestoga wagon and head west, joining that year's convoy of California-bound immigrants. And on July 20, you and the rest of these early pioneers find yourselves staring at a crossroads in what is today southwest Wyoming. Like them, you'll face a choice: Turn right or turn left?

Both trails lead to California, but the trail to the right detours far north. It meanders deep into Idaho before it reverses course and turns back south into eastern Nevada. The left trail, on the other hand, eschews the northern deviation. It takes a straight shot across Utah, and by doing so removes almost 350 miles from

---

*If you want to really strike it rich, forget your gold pan and bring your sewing needle. The real pot of gold in the Gold Rush is selling sturdy denim trousers.

your journey. So let's say you look at a map, you note the more efficient route, and you turn left.

Initially, your choice will seem like the wise one. Lansford Hastings, an adventurer and respected guide, had just scouted this shortcut on horseback the winter before and advertised his new cutoff in guidebooks and postings along the trail. Nevertheless, most of the convoy turn right. They're fearful of the unknown and unwilling to trust one person's word. But you're not. And you're not the only one keen to arrive early in California. When you turn left on that July morning, twenty other wagons do the same. After a few uneventful days, you and the rest of these previously unconnected pioneers caravan together for safety. Following some debate, you'll elect a nice, wealthy, older fellow as the leader of your party.

His name is George Donner.

The problem with the Hastings trail is that there is no trail. It is just a line he drew on a map, and the line runs right over Utah's Wasatch Mountains. Without a wagon road, you'll spend the next thirty-six miles carving one yourself with ax and shovel. You planned for the crossing of the Wasatch to take three days. Instead, it takes three weeks.

On August 20, exhausted and already low on supplies, you'll reach the peak of the Wasatch only to be greeted by a sickening view: the Great Salt Lake Desert. Hastings will have prepared you for this "dry drive," but he said it would be a manageable forty miles. In reality, the distance is more like eighty. At first you'll fear for your cattle's lives. Then you'll fear for your own. For six days and six nights you drive those parched cattle across the desert in a desperate sprint for water.

When you finally reach the other side, your party will have lost three wagons and a quarter of its oxen. Recriminations begin, tensions fray. When you hit a second desert in Nevada, an argument breaks out between your fellow travelers James Reed and John Snyder. Reed stabs Snyder to death, and the party banishes him.* Two days later, Lewis Keseberg kicks a Mr. Hardkoop out of his wagon to lighten his load, leaving him to die.

The Hastings cutoff costs you lives, friends, wagons, food, supplies, tools, livestock—and your most precious asset of all: time. Instead of cutting three weeks from your journey, the Hastings route adds almost four. So rather than rolling safely into Sacramento on October 13, you instead arrive in what is today Reno, Nevada, and prepare for your mountain ascent into the Sierra Nevada.

As tardy as you are, you would still, in a normal year, be fine. Late October and even early November is early for heavy snow in these mountains. In a typical year, the pass wouldn't see heavy snow for another few weeks. "Ninety percent of the time, the Donner Party would have made it," explains Mark McLaughlin, a historian of the Sierra Nevada and author of *The Donner Party: Weathering the Storm.*

Unfortunately, the winter of 1846 starts early. Two weeks of snow have already buried the top of the Sierras when you arrive, and the weather's terrible turn is as unlucky as it is decisive. Your oxen would struggle even in ideal conditions. But when you attempt it on November 1, you'll find the pass buried in five feet of powder. Passage is impossible. So, less than three miles from the summit, you face two terrible options: 1) abandon your wagons and cattle, fashion snowshoes, and trek for Sacramento and your

---

*Which probably saves his life—the Donner Party is an excellent one to be disinvited from—but his banishment may save yours as well. Reed will eventually become the chief organizer of the rescue party.

DONNER PARTY ROUTE

JULY 20, 1846—SPRING 1847

Don't turn left!

California/Oregon Trail

The wrong choice
July 20, 1846

Hasting's "Shortcut"

life; or 2) retreat to a few cabins by Truckee Lake that previous pioneers constructed a few years prior.

The Donners chose to retreat.

When I ask Bill Bowness, a historian at Donner Memorial State Park, whether you should do the same, he tells me he believes fewer Donners would have died had they abandoned their gear and made the trek. So he recommends you go for it. But others, like McLaughlin, aren't so sure. For one thing, a large snowstorm hits the Sierra in the first week of November. And for another, a later attempt by some of the party to snowshoe from Truckee Lake to Sutter's Fort in Sacramento suggests the trip could take as long as a month. If you try to hike out, you'll likely run out of food, probably suffer frostbite, and potentially die from exposure. So choose to play it safe: Retreat to the lake along with the rest of the Donner Party and hole up in those cabins. Just be aware that, by doing so, you're condemning yourself to a winter in the mountains. The Donner Party did not know this. They believed the Sierra, like the mountains they knew in the Midwest, would clear once the weather passed. They did not.

Food soon becomes a problem. You can try to hunt, but this is largely hopeless, since the large animals either evacuate the mountains or hibernate in winter. The only animals that remain are too small to shoot, Bowness tells me, though you could possibly trap them. Moses Schallenberger, a seventeen-year-old pioneer, survived the winter of 1844 alone in the Sierras by trapping coyote and fox (coyote tastes terrible, he later said, but fox is delicious).

Unfortunately, while the Donners were strong, smart, hardworking, entrepreneurial, and industrious, they were midwestern farmers, not mountain men. They didn't have traps, nor did they have the fishing gear to catch trout from the lake. If you're going to eat, it's going to have to be the oxen and the food that came with you in the wagons.

Your food stores last only days. After that, you'll eat your oxen. But after just six weeks at the lake, the leather clothes, boots, and blankets are all the food that remains. You can boil the leather for hours until it turns into a pulp, allow it to cool, and then eat the resulting glue-like substance. But this is starvation food, and you are starving to death.

Soon you'll begin to experience small but noticeable signs of physical and cognitive decline. Your brain will switch its energy source from glucose to fats, and you'll feel increasingly irritable, low energy, and cold as you lose the ability to efficiently constrict your blood vessels. Without food, your body consumes itself for the energy it needs. It starts with the proteins and fats, but because you've already lost so much weight it soon harvests its own muscle, including your heart. Once you lose 35 percent of your body weight, you may experience convulsions and hallucinations. Your weakened heart will develop an arrhythmia and eventually fail.

Exactly how long it takes your body to reach these grim milestones depends on a few important factors: how much you move, how much you eat, your age, your relationship status, and, most important, your sex.

If you're a twentysomething single male in peak physical shape—you're in extreme danger. You have the least fat reserves, the highest metabolism, and no one to help you. Young men in good shape with no families die first in starvation situations. If that describes you, and you don't follow the steps below, you'll be dead by Christmas—much like Baylis Williams, Jacob Donner, Samuel Shoemaker, Joseph Reinhardt, James Smith, and Charles Burger, who all died in the final ten days of December. All of them were men and all—except Donner, who was fifty-six—were between the ages of twenty-four and thirty-six. You'll bury them in shallow, icy graves just outside the cabins.

I asked Donald Grayson, a professor of anthropology at the University of Washington and author of *Sex and Death on the Western Emigrant Trail*, why young men starve the fastest. He said they're at risk for a few reasons. The first is cultural.

The gender roles of 1800s pioneers were clear: "It was the expectation of the men at the time that they would perform the heavy labor, and that's exactly what happened," Grayson says. Hard work increases your caloric needs. So in a cruel twist, the more you help out around camp, and the more you work to carve the trail over the Wasatch, the faster you die.

If you're a woman, you're in less immediate danger than a

man, but that's not only thanks to cultural advantages. You have a few biological ones as well. Women on average have less lean mass than men and more subcutaneous fat, which means their bodies have more stored calories and a lower natural metabolism. In other words, if you're a woman, you have more fuel and better mileage than a man. That matters when you are a long way from a gas station.

This advantage will not only prolong your survival at camp, but will also give you an opportunity for escape that a man would be ill-advised to pursue: On December 16, ten men and five women fashion snowshoes and make a desperate scramble over the pass.

The trip is hellish. They lose their way. They spend a week trapped by a blizzard. They hike for another five freezing weeks with almost no food. But while eight of the ten men who set off die, all five women survive. So, if you're a woman, you can consider escaping with the December 16 group—though the trip will be so awful it's difficult to recommend. If you're a man: hard pass.

Instead, not only should you skip the arduous hike, you should do nothing at all. You need to flatline your metabolism. If you reduce your movement, you can reduce your caloric requirements by some 50 to 80 percent. Rather than working to survive, you want to be in the worst shape of your life. "On the Donner Party, you absolutely want to be a couch potato, not a marathoner," Grayson says. As proof, he points to the example of George Donner, who had a hand infection that kept him bedridden throughout the winter. He survived well into March, long after most men his age had already starved.

By avoiding exercise entirely, and by skipping the starvation hike, you should survive at least into January. But by the first week of February, with salvation still at least three weeks away, you have eaten almost nothing for over a month, and your situation becomes perilous. In the late days of January and the first week of February, John Landrum Murphy, Augustus Spitzer, Milt Elliot, and Eleanor Eddy—the first woman to starve to death—all die by the lake. If you don't find something to eat, you may soon join them. Fortunately, there's food all around you. You'll just have to overcome a powerful taboo to eat it.

Eating human flesh hasn't always been so distasteful. At least not socially. Archaeologists have found butchered human bones far too frequently for it to have been a sporadic, starvation-only practice. And before Western culture washed over the globe, ritualistic cannibalism was not uncommon.

In the Amazon rainforest, the indigenous Wari' people "were just as mortified to learn that Westerners were burying their dead as the Westerners were to learn that the Wari' were eating theirs," Bill Schutt, author of *Cannibalism: A Perfectly Natural History*, tells me.

In other words, the revulsion to cannibalism is not innate. It's a societal taboo without a Darwinian explanation (such as there is against incest).* What sets cannibalism apart from other social taboos is its remarkable power. The Donner Party might be infamous for its cannibalism, but more than a dozen members of the party opted to starve to death rather than eat the human dead.

When I ask Schutt how the cannibalism taboo became so strong that a person might die rather than break it, he says the explanation is partly due to its antiquity. People have feared and despised cannibals for so long that it may feel as if you're breaking some law of nature when you break off a rib. But what you're

---

*In fact, there's good reason to believe natural selection should have selected for cannibalism rather than against it. After all, when practiced appropriately, it can save lives. It's about to save yours.

actually doing is breaking a social norm invented by a few xeno-phobic Ancient Greeks, according to Schutt.

Schutt has traced the earliest examples of the taboo in Western culture to some of the earliest known Greek stories, such as the tale of Polyphemus and Odysseus in Homer's *Odyssey*. In the story of Polyphemus, the Cyclops catches Odysseus and his men steal-ing from him and begins to eat them one by one until Odysseus blinds the giant.[*] It may be the first example of a writer depicting cannibalism as the act of a monster, according to Schutt. But it would hardly be the last.

"The Greeks used cannibalism as a way to define the worst be-havior possible in another group," Schutt tells me. The probable explanation for why they chose cannibalism as the act of a mon-ster is fairly straightforward: It's what their northern European enemies, the Androphagi (Greek for "man-eaters"), did. For the Greeks, human flesh was the food of foreigners—and thus eating it the lowest one could stoop. From there, the stigma only grew.

"The Romans took the taboo from the Greeks, where it com-bined with Judeo-Christian beliefs about how you treat the dead," Schutt says. Combine that with the racism of early anthropolo-gists, who used its practice as justification to commit cultural genocide, and the stigma compounded to such an extent that many in the Donner Party died rather than break it. No cannibal-ism took place among the Donner Party members trapped by the lake until late February, after at least thirteen people had starved to death.[†]

---

[*]Homer may have invented the trope, but he was far from the last to use it. See zombies, *Dracula*, *Hansel and Gretel*, *Little Red Riding Hood*, *Snow White*, and basically every other story told by the Brothers Grimm.

[†]The hikers on the December attempt to hike out did eat Franklin Ward Graves, Antonio (last name unknown), Patrick Dolan, and Jay Fosdick after they died. There's also reason to believe one of the hikers, a man named Wil-liam Foster, shot two Native Miwok guides named Louis and Salvador for food,

Don't be one of them. There is frozen food buried by the lake. If you want to survive, you need to eat it. All you have to do is grab a knife, a shovel, and overcome an old xenophobic taboo. According to a gruesome experiment in the early 1900s by the journalist William Seabrook, it tastes like veal.

The calories will keep you alive, and for far longer than you might expect. Of those who eventually cannibalized, Keseberg appears to have done so with the most vigor. He not only survived but, for reasons unknown, skipped the first two rescue parties and yet was still alive and strong enough to hike out with the third on April 17.

When practicing cannibalism, there are a few safety precautions one must take. First, cook your meat thoroughly to avoid diseases. No tartares or carpaccios. Also, avoid the brain. You run a small risk of catching a deadly prion disease called kuru from eating it. Instead, target the thighs, butt, calves, and back muscles for the highest caloric returns. At 32,000 calories per body (based on a 145-pound male body, which, while light, may be accurate in this case, since you're eating people who've starved), and at least thirteen bodies, there will be plenty of food for you to eat and even share until the arrival of the first rescue party on February 18.

After eight days of hiking in deep snow, you'll arrive at a forward camp in Bear Valley and a pantry full of delicious food. Don't eat it. Or at least, don't eat very much. Starvation has dropped minerals like phosphate and magnesium to dangerously low levels in your body, and because digestion draws those minerals from your blood, eating in your state could actually kill you. William Hook, who hiked out with the first rescue party, gorged himself and died. So nibble, don't splurge, and you can survive.

which is the only instance anyone in the Donner Party was killed and eaten. The rest of the cannibalized were already dead.

Even if you join the Donner Party, you can arrive safely in California. Just move as little as possible, skip the snowshoeing group, learn to love pulpy leather food—and, of course, overcome an age-old taboo handed down by a few xenophobic Ancient Greeks.

Or you can just turn right.

HOW TO SURVIVE
THE 1906 EARTHQUAKE

Let's say you want to go on a walking tour of San Francisco at the city's warmest and most energetic. You want to see the port town after the rush for gold swelled the foggy backwater into the largest city west of the Mississippi—back when it was home to the West Coast's tallest buildings, and before modern movements replaced its beautiful brick architecture. You want to see the city as it was before the Golden Gate Bridge sutured California's great gap, back when escaping the peninsula meant waiting for the ferry.

So you travel back to April 18, 1906, and because you have a big day ahead of you, you arrive in the early morning hours, while most of the city still sleeps and gas-powered lamps provide the street's only light.

Because you've done your research, you appropriately begin your walking tour in the location of the city's founding: the Mission San Francisco de Asís, also known as the Mission Dolores, established when the Spanish missionary Francisco Palóu first arrived on the sandy, hilly, isolated peninsula in 1776.

When Francisco named the church, he did so after the Dolores Creek that flowed by the old mission. That may surprise you. As you look around, you don't see a creek. But the old creek bed is there, buried beneath the street by a mixture of sod and trash infill thrown there by the pioneers, who dumped garbage and dirt into the marsh so they could build on top of it. Roads, churches, stockyards, and housing obscure the old muddy pit, but it's there, forming the foundations of the buildings looming above you. And just as you're absorbing this odd, obscure, random-seeming geologic fact, at exactly 5:12 in the morning you feel a sharp, sudden jolt beneath your feet.

It's startling.

It's harmless.

It's a warning.

You need to run.

The jolt is a foreshock. It's the first wave of energy passing through the earth's crust that presages the main event. The main event, in this case, is the biggest earthquake to ever hit a major U.S. city. Survivor testimony suggests the foreshock arrived approximately thirty seconds before the real shaking began, which means you have roughly thirty seconds to find shelter before a 7.8-magnitude earthquake slams into a city woefully unprepared for it. Many buildings collapse. Nearly every building sustains serious damage. Bricks, church steeples, balconies, and towers shower down on the streets below. Water mains burst. Gas mains explode, and nearly everything not shaken to the ground burns in the subsequent four-day firestorm that incinerates an area twice the size of the Great Chicago Fire. In the long history of American natural disasters, the 1906 quake compares only to the 1900 Galveston hurricane in terms of lives lost. In terms of economic damage, there is no comparison at all. Over the next four

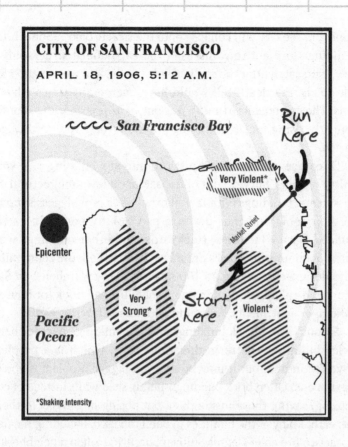

CITY OF SAN FRANCISCO

APRIL 18, 1906, 5:12 A.M.

San Francisco Bay

Run Here

Very Violent*

Market Street

Epicenter

Very Strong*

Start Here

Violent*

Pacific Ocean

*Shaking intensity

days three quarters of the city crumbles into rubble and ash. At least 300,000 people are left homeless. More than 3,000 die.

But all that comes later.

At first, when you feel the foreshock, you need to get off the street, because you're surrounded by buildings of dubious construction with foundations wobbling atop an old pioneer trash pit. Oddly, the safest course of action is to get inside one. The only place more dangerous than inside a wobbly building is beside one, because in thirty seconds nearly every chimney, church spire, and cupola in the city will collapse onto the streets below. Some brick buildings lose entire walls. Had the earthquake struck only a few hours later, after the city had come to life and workers flooded the roads, the death toll would have been many times what it was. The earthquake's timing was one of its few charities, but for an early rising tourist it's doing you no favors. You need to get inside.

Of course, you shouldn't just run into any building. Use your thirty seconds. Survey your options. Make a few architectural assessments. Buildings with few interior walls provide less support to their roofs and thus perform particularly poorly in earthquakes. Barns, factories, stockyards, and other buildings with large open interior spaces are more likely to collapse than buildings designed for living. In 1906, nearly every warehouse in San Francisco collapsed. So don't go in one. Instead, look for houses, offices, or apartments. Anything with lots of interior walls.

Second, avoid brick buildings *and* the buildings next to them. Brick buildings shatter rather than sway, which is a problem if you're in one, but it may be an even bigger problem if you're next to one. Often brick buildings merely shed walls instead of collapsing, saving those inside them but posing huge risks to those beneath. Many of the fatalities in San Francisco, including the San Francisco fire chief Dennis Sullivan, occurred when a neighboring building collapsed onto their otherwise stable roof.

Finally, when choosing a building, take a second to note its orientation. Surprisingly, the direction it faces matters. If you can, run into a building with a foundation oriented north-south, rather than east-west. It will be far more stable in the upcoming east-to-west shift.

Once you've found the perfectly oriented, single-story, multi-room, wood-frame house with similarly constructed neighbors, get beneath a doorway or at the very least hide beneath a table. Crouch low, cover your head with your arms, and, if you can, look to your west, where a tiny piece of the San Andreas Fault the size of a dinner plate has has just broken free.

The San Andreas Fault marks the meeting point between the massive tectonic plates supporting the Pacific Ocean and North America. Unlike the Cascadia fault zone to the north, neither plate slides beneath the other. Instead, while the two plates both move in the same northwest direction, the Pacific plate moves faster, and thus their movement is far from harmonious. Friction can hold the plates together for decades or even centuries. But as the years pass, the strain builds until, like an avalanche on a snow-laden mountain, one small disturbance sets off a massive chain reaction.

At twelve minutes past five in the morning on April 18, 1906, a small section of the San Andreas fault line broke just west of the soon-to-be-built Golden Gate Bridge. William Ellsworth, professor of geophysics at Stanford University, tells me the initial break occurred in a section of the fault as small as a dinner plate. These types of snaps occur all the time as the two faults grind against each other. But it so happened that this time, after centuries of built tension, the tiny snap cascaded into what was nearly the most powerful quake the San Andreas Fault is capable of producing. In a moment, the Pacific plate snapped north by an average of fifteen feet relative to its North American partner. In some places, it leaped by as much as twenty.

The rupture raced down the fault at nearly two miles per second. It moved north, crossed back onto land just west of San Rafael, ran beneath Marin, Petaluma, Santa Rosa, and continued farther north until it stopped just short of Eureka—a distance of more than 200 miles.

The rupture also moved south. It passed through the hills of southern San Francisco, under the San Andreas reservoir for which the fault is named, down through what would become Silicon Valley, through San Jose, Salinas, and all the way to San Luis Obispo. In total, the quake ripped apart nearly 300 miles of the California coastline.

The sudden jolt sent powerful pressure waves rippling outward through the earth like the wake cast off a speeding motorboat. Successive three-foot earthen undulations moved through the earth's crust at nine times the speed of sound. They rocked, compressed, and shattered the soil as they radiated away from the rupture site.

The crew of the *Argo*, a steamer headed for the San Francisco Bay, were the first to feel the jolt. Bolts blasted out of their sockets and the solid metal hull dented inward, as if a depth charge had gone off in close proximity. The captain later said it felt as if the whole ship were breaking apart. The crew scrambled out of their bunks, expecting to see a rock or rogue wave. Instead, they saw nothing but blue, flat water, with no tsunami or even wave in sight. Fortunately for the *Argo*, strike-slip fault lines like San Andreas do not typically produce large tsunamis. Their side-to-side movement rattles the earth but doesn't displace the huge quantities of water required to produce massive waves. Instead, tsunamis usually occur in earthquakes along subduction plates, when one plate subsumes another. There, when the fault ruptures, the seabed drops. In the 2011 quake that sent the 120-foot-high tsunami toward Japan, the ocean floor fell more than fifty feet. Because the San Andreas shakes side to side, it displaces little water, even in its largest ruptures, which is why, though you face many dangers in 1906, you need not worry about tsunamis.

Within seconds of the rupture, earthen swells pass through San Francisco. If you continue to look westward, you may even see them coming. You may first see the tops of buildings begin to dance against the sky. The St. Francis Hotel shakes so violently it looks like "a tree in a tempest," according to one journalist's account. Shortly afterward, you may even see the waves themselves pass like supersonic sea swells. Jesse Cook, a police sergeant working downtown, said the undulations looked "as if the waves of the ocean were coming towards me, billowing as they came."

As the waves arrive, so does the sound—a deep, horrible rumble and screech as rock grinds into rock, cement cracks, foundations crumble, and bricks cascade down from above. As the rupture passes through the hilly neighborhoods of San Francisco to your north and west, the sturdy bedrock mutes the earth's motion. According to a damage assessment conducted by the seismologist Harry O. Wood shortly after the earthquake, the shaking on San Francisco's bedrock never exceeds a VII out of X on the Rossi-Forel intensity scale. But down where you are, sitting atop the porous landfill of the old pioneers, you may as well be sitting on a bowl of Jell-O. The soft soil behaves like a liquid, sloshing back and forth between the troughs and peaks of the repeated waves. On the Rossi-Forel scale, the shaking reaches IX. If you're standing, you'll be knocked to the ground and pinned there "as if glued," recalled Sergeant Cook. On the other side of the city, a four-year-old Ansel Adams falls and breaks his nose, "forever marring my beauty," he later said.

If you want to avoid a similar fate—or worse—tuck into a ball, cover your head and neck with your arms, and wait as successive three-foot earthen waves rip the soft soil apart, compacting and settling the loose dirt with each passing swell. In less than a minute, the Mission District of San Francisco snaps south seven feet and drops another five. Some buildings withstand the shift, but many do not.

The earthquake exposes San Francisco's history of corrupt politics and reckless construction like a scrupulous inspector. It tests the city's cheaply constructed boardinghouses built with extreme hubris atop the trash and soft soil of San Francisco's formerly marshy districts near the water, and finds many wanting. Even City Hall collapses, a result of mixing "bad politics and bad cement," the Chamber of Commerce later says. The Valencia Street Hotel telescopes into the ground so completely that the residents of the top story walk out the doors onto street level, while those in the lower stories die in the crush. The brick church beside the Mission Dolores falls in on itself. The walls of the Columbia Theatre and the Valencia Hotel collapse into their neighbors, crushing the smaller buildings.

After sixty seconds of relentless shaking, the earthquake and its deafening cacophony finally end, allowing you to hear a quieter, even more horrifying sound: the soft hiss of escaping gas.

Let's say you pick the right building, you survive, and, almost as important, you aren't trapped. That's good. But the danger has only just begun, and now you need to leave your lifesaving shelter as quickly as you ran in. The shifting earth has compacted the gas mains running north-south beneath the city roads. If you look onto the street, you may seem them poking above the ground like the bones of a fractured arm. These severed mains now spew their gas into arcing electrical lines, and underground explosions go off like cord charges down the street, excavating deep trenches. Days later, these trenches will be filled with the thousands of dead horses and stockyard animals killed by falling debris. But for now, the explosions ignite the city's traditional tinderbox: the densely packed clapboard housing south of Market Street. Within minutes, no fewer than fifty fires burn throughout San Francisco's southern districts.

Fire was a familiar foe to the citizens of San Francisco. At least seven major fires ravaged the city during its Gold Rush era of growth, including a three-day firestorm in 1851 that destroyed three quarters of its structures. Fire ripped through the city so frequently that some locals living in the fire-prone district South of Market had rebuilt their homes and businesses as many as five separate times.

Just a year before the earthquake, the National Board of Fire Underwriters conducted an analysis of San Francisco's susceptibility to fire and concluded that its combination of tall buildings, high winds, density, and wood construction created a fire hazard it qualified as "alarmingly severe." The report found that San Francisco's 548 uniformed firefighters would be hard-pressed to defend the city against a dozen simultaneous fires. By 5:30 a.m. on April 18, 1906, they faced at least fifty.

A postmortem report of the 1906 firestorms conducted by the NBFU concluded the conflagrations would have overwhelmed the city's fire department even under ideal conditions. But what little chance they did have went up like so much smoke when the firefighters attached their hoses to the hydrants and discovered the gas mains weren't the only underground pipes to snap in the quake. In the early, critical minutes after the fires first began, firefighters had almost no access to water anywhere in the city. Later examinations revealed that the matrix of plumbing pipes connecting the city to its nine district reservoirs snapped in at least 20,000 places. Water from the cracked piping spewed into the streets and houses, drowned those trapped in collapsed buildings, and drained the district reservoirs so that nary a drop of water ran through San Francisco just when its firefighters needed it most.

Fortunately for you, the first fires ignite to your south and east, which means you have some time. Once you run out of your building and back onto the streets of the Mission, you'll find absolute chaos. Hard experience has taught the people of San Francisco the danger even distant fires pose, and as soon as black smoke begins rising across the eastern horizon, the evacuation will commence. You'll see half-dressed businessmen with faces covered in shaving cream, families carrying all they can hold, and business owners saving their most valuable wares. James Hopper, writing for the *San Francisco Call*, reports seeing a barefoot man in pink pajamas, pink bathrobe, wrapped in a pink comforter stylishly making his escape.

In 1906 no bridge yet connects the San Francisco Peninsula to the rest of the Bay Area. Fortunately, in the face of the fires, every boat in the bay—from tugboats to cargo ships to private sailboats—mounts a Dunkirk-like evacuation from the city's wharfs. By the end of the fire, these boats will evacuate more than 30,000 people across the bay. You need to be one of them.

Many of the boats depart from the Ferry Building, where Market Street tees into the bay. Market is just a few blocks to your north, so get out onto Mission Street and turn left. But as you move north, check behind you. There's a rather surprising but very lethal threat stampeding from your south.

In the immediate aftermath of the earthquake, some sixty longhorn cattle escaped from a collapsed stockyard just to your south. For a brief moment, Pamplona comes to San Francisco. The bulls stampede down Mission Street, trample panicked residents, and gore the saloon owner John Moller before he can squeeze back into his establishment. As you run, keep checking for steer—and move faster than the poor Mr. Moller when you see them coming.

After a few blocks you'll arrive on Market Street, which is San Francisco's answer to New York's Broadway. The wide main boulevard cuts diagonally through the city, stretching from the peninsula's geographic center to the bay. Look to your right down the long boulevard and you'll see a building's tall tower at the end, two and a half miles away. That's your goal. Fire will eventually close this escape route, but not until the early afternoon. If you move, you should make it before then.

However, you shouldn't sprint or even run. Move deliberately, pay attention to passing police or soldiers, and if they give you any instructions, follow them.

Fire and cattle are not the only dangers here.

In the minutes after the earthquake, less than a mile from you but standing high up on the relative safety of the sturdy bedrock beneath the Russian Hill neighborhood, the Brigadier General Frederick Funston surveys the chaos unfolding below. Funston serves as the commanding officer of the Presidio military fort in the north of the city. He is a veteran of both the Spanish-American and Philippine-American Wars and received a Medal of Honor in the latter for attacking an enemy's fortified position in a raft. He is, as they say of good army men at this time, a man of action. He isn't about to let an ignorance of firefighting techniques, an utter lack of experience in city government, a military tradition dating back to the Magna Carta, or the United States Constitution prevent him from taking control of a chaotic situation.

So, standing atop that hill at about the same time you're dodging a steer's horns, General Funston concludes that the situation, the city, and its citizens require the full weight of his experience. At 5:30 a.m. he illegally enacts martial law of his own accord and orders his garrisoned troops into the city with bayonets fixed. By 7 a.m., the largest peacetime military occupation of a U.S. city in history marches into the streets of San Francisco under direct orders to shoot anyone suspected of looting.

Many of the soldiers follow their illegal orders all too closely and incuriously. Suspicion is enough for a death sentence. Soldiers fire on anyone running out of a building with their arms full—even when the building is seconds from incineration—without asking any questions, including seemingly important ones, like whether the person owns the business and is trying to save their own stuff.

No one knows the exact number of citizens shot by Funston's soldiers over the four-day firestorm. But contemporary newspaper accounts concluded the soldiers and police shot or stabbed at least a hundred suspected "looters." With the destruction of City Hall, most of the victims remain anonymous. But the name and circumstances of death of at least one person is known: the prominent San Francisco businessman Heber C. Tilden. He was working for the Red Cross when soldiers shot him after he accidentally drove past a checkpoint.

As you walk down Market, don't go into any buildings and keep your arms completely empty and your eyes off the fleeing bankers as they evacuate wheelbarrows of cash and carts of gold. You're walking close to the patrolling soldiers and the first reported shooting, which occurs on Market Street just after 7 a.m., when soldiers shoot a man in the back as he flees a building with his arms full. Fire quickly incinerates his abandoned body along with any evidence of who he was or what he was doing.

By the time you make it halfway down Market, the separate streams of smoke rising from the dense neighborhoods to your south will have coalesced into a single, towering black cloud. By now, fire has consumed the crowded clapboard housing of the working-class district and built itself into an inferno so hot and close it has developed its own wind system.

The heat in the fire's center will by now exceed 2,000 degrees, warming so much air so quickly that it ascends in powerful thermals at speeds in excess of 80 miles per hour. Like a thunderstorm of fire, the hot air rises some six miles high, cools in the high atmosphere, and rockets downward, creating vortices from the wind shear and small tornadoes of flame.

With its own wind fanning its flames, urban firestorms flood their surroundings with spark showers that fire experts call an "ember attack." Even buildings of brick and other seemingly flameproof materials succumb to the onslaught. Sparks probe their every crevice, hunting for a way into their flammable interior. Inevitably, the embers find purchase. They snake through ventilation systems, pass through open windows, or find cracks in the construction. Once inside, flames consume the buildings from the inside out, leaving nothing behind but burned-out husks.

Despite the fire being blocks away, you'll still feel its heat. A patrolman guarding the nearby San Francisco Mint later said he was worried about looters until about midday. After that, he said, the heat grew so intense that "the devil himself couldn't have come very close."

As soon as their hydrants fail, the fire department gives up any hope of extinguishing the fire directly. Instead, they build a fire line along Market Street, hoping to contain the blaze to the city's southern districts. To assist their efforts and widen the firebreak, the department, with the assistance of the military, turn to explosives.

It does not go well.

They detonate the first of many San Francisco buildings at 9 a.m. that morning. You might even see it off the corner of Sixth and Market. Don't stop to watch. The soldiers who set the fuse misjudge the timing, and one of them, Lieutenant Charles Pulis, dies in the blast. It's the first tragic failure of what would turn out to be a disastrous strategy that only serves to ignite buildings, start fires behind fire lines, and destroy the city.

As you move down Market, you'll hear increasingly frequent explosions above the roar of the flames. In some cases, you may even see bombs going off in buildings already lit by fire or, in one spectacularly disastrous case, when soldiers detonate a fireworks factory near the water.

Any hope the fire department had of holding the fire line at Market Street ends by 9:30 a.m., when a new fire begins in a kitchen on the corner of Hayes and Gough Streets, deep behind the firebreak. "Had there been the slightest quantity of water attainable when this fire was discovered it would have been easily extinguished," a responding firefighter later says. "But we were compelled to watch it burn and spread."

The fire forces firefighters to retreat to their secondary fire line. Just before noon the fire crosses the northern end of Market Street and burns the banks on California Street, the Italian district of North Beach, and Chinatown. But if you keep moving, you should arrive at the Ferry Building before fire seals the path behind you.

Once you reach the Ferry Building, you have a choice. You can depart on one of the many boats leaving for Oakland or Alcatraz Island (don't worry; it's not a federal prison yet).

Or you can stay and help the only successful firefighting effort the city ever mounts.

At about the same time you arrive at the Ferry Building, so does a navy lieutenant by the name of Frederick Freeman, along with sixty-six sailors, a destroyer, and two firefighting tugs. The tugs come equipped with powerful pumps, and they soon provide some of the only water in the entire city.

Over the next seventy consecutive hours, Freeman and his sailors will fight the fires along the waterfront. As the rest of the city burns, and as General Funston ineffectively detonates hundreds of buildings in a failed attempt to establish a second fire line along Van Ness Avenue, Freeman keeps the piers open, allowing boats to continue to ferry evacuees to safety. You can join him, and over the next four days help save the lives of hundreds of San Franciscans.

After four days, the fires will finally burn out in the sandy dunes of San Francisco's western edge. You can then, if you'd like, safely finish your tour—though, according to the novelist Jack London, there may not be much to see. London walked the city shortly after the disaster as a journalist for *Collier's* magazine and wrote: "Not in history has a modern imperial city been so completely destroyed. San Francisco is gone."

So it may be a good time to end your visit instead. Of course, the San Andreas Fault still runs beneath San Francisco, it's still active, and after all these years no technology yet exists to predict earthquakes. The best geologists can do is use the frequency of a fault's great ruptures to gauge when it might happen again. According to the United States Geological Survey, the San Andreas Fault averages a 1906-sized earthquake every 200 years. So you may not need to visit this disaster. Instead, it might visit you.

HOW TO SURVIVE

THE SINKING OF THE *TITANIC*

Let's say you want to embark on a refreshing cruise into remote seas aboard a ship with a touch of early twentieth-century elegance. So you travel to Southampton, England, on April 10, 1912, and you buy a ticket to New York City on the new state-of-the-art cruise liner from White Star Line headed out on its maiden voyage. But you're a frugal time traveler, so you elect to travel third class—only £8! That buys you a bunk on F deck, six levels below the top. It's about the size of a prison cell, only it's occupied by four people rather than just two.

But who cares! All you'll do is sleep in it anyway, and this ship offers world-class amenities to its third-class passengers, who in this era would typically have to stuff themselves into one large, poorly ventilated and inadequately converted cargo hold. Here you'll enjoy the relative privacy of a shared bunk, the open air via the lower poop deck, and even have access to the third-class saloon.

The first few days of the trip pass unremarkably. You'll venture to the back poop deck for some fresh air, play a card game in the saloon, and then, perhaps in a fit of boredom, finally bother to read the fine print on your ticket. There you'll discover, just beneath the big bold letters WHITE STAR LINE, the name of your vessel: R.M.S. TITANIC.

Don't panic. You still have a few days before the infamous accident, and you need to use them. In the bowels of the *Titanic*, you'll face a number of daunting obstacles—including logistics, discrimination, and chaos—but the first and perhaps most important problem is one of simple navigation. As a third-class passenger, you're not allowed access to the top deck. That isn't only a matter of inconvenience. It's where the lifeboats are. And while there is an escape path, it's locked, unlabeled, and there have been no escape drills. Most third-class passengers on *Titanic* have no idea how to navigate the unlabeled labyrinth of passageways, stairwells, and ladders to reach the lifeboats. You'll need to learn. Forget the card games and fresh air. You need to familiarize yourself with the bowels of this ship. Study the deck plan, climb the stairwells, walk the corridors, and if you happen to see a crew member while doing so, perhaps suggest the boat slow down. Because as it is, *Titanic* is navigating icebergs off the coast of Newfoundland at far too great a speed.

At 11:40 p.m. on the moonless night of April 14, 1912, *Titanic*'s lookouts Frederick Fleet and Reginald Lee first spotted the 1.5-million-ton block of ice when it was only 500 yards in front of the ship. The *Titanic*, unlike ships in the Royal Navy, steamed without spotlights, so even though the massive block of ice rose more than 100 feet above the water, it remained camouflaged against the dark sky until it was far too late. When Fleet first rang the helm, the 50,000-ton ship was barreling through the North Atlantic sea at 22 knots. At that speed, it was only thirty-seven seconds from impact.

At the call of iceberg, *Titanic* reversed its engines and executed a hard left turn, but there was not nearly enough time. The maneuver avoided a head-on impact, but at 11:41 p.m. *Titanic* scraped 300 feet of its front starboard side against the ice.

Sleeping on F deck, you'll be one of the closest passengers to the impact, but even so the jolt will feel relatively benign. Perhaps even anticlimactic. One fireman bunked within feet of the collision later claimed to have slept through the incident entirely. "Dead to the wide [world]," he told investigators. Other, lighter sleepers will describe the impact as a "big vibration," "a large cable being run out," "a grinding crash," "crunching and jarring," or like "a basket of coals dumped on an iron plate."

Because the lurch is so mild, few passengers initially suspect a serious problem. But of course, there is a serious problem. You're six decks below the lifeboats while seven tons of water pour into the lower holds every second. You need to act.

Your first instinct might be to immediately sprint out of your bunk. Don't. You have plenty of time before water floods your section of the ship, and you need to use that time wisely. Instead of running, change into your finest clothing. Put on a tux, a dress, or at the very least brush your hair. The lifeboats load from the first-class deck, which means for a brief but critical period they are an invitation-only party you need to crash. It will help if you look the part. Finally, before you depart, put on the life jacket stored above your bunk.

Getting dressed will take a few extra minutes, but don't worry. The great ship sinks so slowly you could make an interminable movie out of its demise. More than two and a half hours will elapse from impact to final foundering. And even more remarkable than the length of its fight against the weight of the frigid north Atlantic sea is the grace with which she fights it. The *Titanic* never capsizes, nor even takes on the kind of serious list that would make navigating the ladders and stairwells difficult or the launch of lifeboats impossible. Remarkably, the *Titanic*'s deck never tilts beyond a few degrees, even as she takes on thousands of tons of water.

As a result, you not only have time to dress yourself, but when you do finally make it to the top decks, you won't find the sheer chaos that accompanies most founderings. Instead, you'll find a sociological cocktail of gallantry, cowardice, courage, chivalry, sacrifice, prayer, panic, and even music. The time *Titanic* takes to sink enables you to escape from even its lowest holds, but it also produces a human drama that partially explains the wreck's infamy.

Ships don't often slide so graciously into the sea, especially at the turn of the twentieth century. This partially explains why *Titanic* carried lifeboats for only a third of its capacity. It wasn't as if *Titanic*'s designers couldn't do the math. They simply never expected anyone would survive a shipwreck long enough to use them. Most ships, particularly in that era, sank catastrophically. They capsized, disintegrated, sank within minutes, or listed to such a degree that passengers could barely walk, let alone launch boats. Ship designers, and even passengers, viewed lifeboats as token nods to safety, akin to how a modern airplane traveler might view their flotation device. It was difficult to envision a scenario where *anyone* might live long enough to use it, let alone everyone. Given the grim realities of nineteenth-century shipwrecks, a ship equipped with lifeboats for a third of it passengers seemed hopelessly aspirational.

But *Titanic*'s architects underestimated their own design. When I asked ship designer and naval architect Jan-Erik Wahl why *Titanic* sank in such an unfathomably sturdy way, he told me it was thanks to the nature of the damage and the ship's use of what was then a state-of-the-art* system of waterproof bulkheads. Bulkheads are

*Bulkheads were state-of-the-art in Western shipping, but Chinese ship designers had used them since at least the fifth century.

waterproof walls that run widthwise across a ship's hull to prevent a single gash from flooding the entire boat. To allow passengers and crew to navigate *Titanic*, the bulkheads had watertight doors that the captain could seal remotely from the bridge. On *Titanic*, the captain closes these doors immediately after impact, but don't worry: You won't be trapped. Bulkheads don't have ceilings—that would introduce the seriously destabilizing possibility of water trapped at the top of the ship. On *Titanic* the bulkheads rise fifty feet from the bottom of the ship, and escape ladders allow sealed-off passengers and crew to climb above them.

Of course, a bulkhead without a ceiling has an obvious weakness: If enough sections flood, the weight of the water will drag the tops of the bulkheads beneath the waterline and render the entire system useless. The height of *Titanic*'s bulkheads meant she could flood four of her forward sections and still float high enough to keep the tops of the bulkheads above water. Unfortunately, the iceberg sliced holes into five. *Titanic* eventually took on 16,000 tons of water, the bow dropped more than fifty feet, seawater flooded over the top of the sixth bulkhead, and as the investigating commissioner later said, "the epitaph of the ship had been written."*

If the bulkheads had been a mere twenty feet taller, the ship

---

*That may not actually be entirely correct. There is a chance you can actually save the ship after it hits the iceberg. It's a small chance. Very small, in fact. And it's remarkably, stupefyingly dangerous. But there is a chance. If you want to try, here's what you need to do: We now know the bulkheads nearly stayed above the waterline, which means if you can prevent approximately 20 percent of the forward compartments from flooding, you may be able to save the ship. Don't bother trying to plug the holes. Even with the help of the entire crew, that would not have worked, according to Wilding. Instead, your best chance would be to fill up the flooding sections with enough bulky, lightweight material to displace the heavier volume of water. One rather risky suggestion, proposed in the National Geographic documentary *Titanic: The Final Word with James Cameron*: Gather all 3,500 life jackets on the ship and stuff them into Boiler Room 6 in under forty minutes. You just might save the ship.

would have likely survived, according to the ship's assistant designer Edward Wilding. As it was, they merely delayed the sinking, by slowing down the flooding between the fifth and sixth bulkheads as the pressure difference between the inside and outside of the ship nearly equalized. For nearly twenty minutes the flooding inflow slowed to a trickle before the water crested the bulkheads and rushed in anew.

The bulkheads don't save the ship, but they do buy you time. Even more critically, they help stabilize the ship's descent. By restricting the water's movement, they reduce what naval architects refer to as the "free surface effect," which is water's dangerously destabilizing desire to pile on the listing side of a ship. Had the ship been open-hulled, flooding water would not only have sunk the ship far faster; it would have flipped the 50,000-ton boat within fifteen minutes, according to Wilding, and no lifeboats would have ever been launched.

Of course, Titanic's slow and steady drop reveal the inequities between passenger classes and the paltry safety precautions taken by the crew. Without any idea of where to go, many third-class passengers move toward the only open-air section of the boat they know: the back poop deck.

Do not do this. Instead, you need to go straight up. You can do so using one of the unannounced evacuation routes. There are two.

The first is a normally locked stairwell off the main third-class alleyway. To find it, move from your bunk on F deck, head toward the rear of the ship, and take the first flight of stairs you see. Climb up the stairs and exit into the main working alleyway on the port side—called Scotland Road. From there, use the escape stairs located behind the elevators (see map below). These doors are normally locked to prevent lower-class passengers from reaching the upper-class decks, but according to testimony by Titanic's head baker, Charles Joughin, they're open sometime between

12:15 and 12:30 a.m. Even if it's the latter, that still gives you ten minutes before the first lifeboat launches.

If for some reason Joughin is wrong and the gate remains locked, you should abandon it and use the other escape route. Your best chance for a seat on a lifeboat is to arrive early, and after 12:30 a.m. you're running short of time.

The secondary escape path is a series of ladders that climb from the forward deck all the way to the top. To get to them, move down the Scotland Road passageway to the forward steerage deck. There on the deck you'll see ladders leading up the successive levels. Normally these are gated and guarded, but a few third-class survivors who used these ladders early in the evening later testified that all the crew members did was ask them not to. Apparently, they ignored them. You should too.

Once you're on the top level, you'll find lifeboats on both the port and starboard sides readying to launch. Which side you use is important, and the best choice depends on your age and gender. *Titanic*'s crew preferentially load women and children into lifeboats, but passenger manifests suggest the crew on the port side follow this policy far more strictly.

At one point Harold Lowe, the officer loading the port-side boats, fires a warning shot from his pistol and declares, "If any man jumps onto the boat I will shoot him like a dog." Clearly, if you're a woman or below the age of thirteen, head straight for Officer Lowe. Otherwise, go to starboard.

If you can catch a ride on one of these first boats—fantastic! You're saved. But sadly, even if you arrive early and even if you're dressed in your finest, there's a good chance you won't. And if you haven't made it onto one of the first boats, your odds dim significantly as more and more people arrive and become increasingly desperate. If you still haven't found a ride by 1:15 a.m., steel your nerves and head back down into the bowels of the sinking ship.

We know from eyewitness testimony that, just after 1 a.m.,

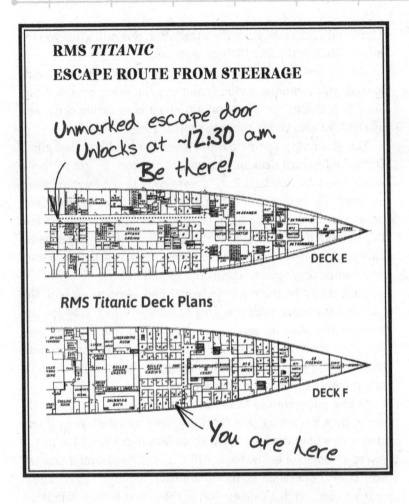

while loading lifeboat 6 to half capacity, Second Officer Charles Lightoller ordered boatswain Alfred Nichols and six other men to go belowdeck and open the gangway doors.* These doors have a

*Lightoller never boarded a lifeboat himself, but he survived the frigid water by swimming onto an overturned raft and waiting until morning for rescue. Almost thirty years later, he aided the English evacuation at Dunkirk by navigating his private sailboat across the English Channel and crowding 127

dual purpose. At port, they allow passengers to directly access the lower decks from the dock, but they also serve as escape doors during an emergency. They were designed to allow steerage passengers to escape into the lifeboats without having to climb to the top deck. It was a good plan, but not only did no one ever tell the passengers, Officer Lightoller was the last person to see Nichols or any of his men alive. Whether Nichols ever opened the gangway doors remains one of the wreck's great mysteries, and no passengers ever escaped through them.

Nevertheless, there is some reason to believe you can. Submersibles examining *Titanic*'s wreckage have found the gangway doors on *Titanic*'s forward port D deck wide open. It's possible flooding water or the tremendous pressure applied by the ocean's depths blew these doors open. But it's also possible that Nichols or one of his men managed to open them before drowning, and they went unused simply because no passengers knew of their existence.

If you arrive at D deck when Nichols does—presumably by 1:30—you may find an open door and a steady stream of half-filled lifeboats. Thomas Jones, the crew member in charge of lifeboat 8, will later testify that he would have rescued passengers at the gangway doors had he seen any. "If they had been down there, we could have taken them," he told the investigating commission. I would suggest you be there.

Of course, because no passengers escape using these doors, the viability of this exit remains somewhat speculative. There's a chance you'll find no Nichols and locked doors. Give him a few minutes, but if the doors aren't open by 1:45 you should wait no longer. Head back up. D deck will soon dip below the waterline.

By this time, your chance for a ride on a lifeboat has gone from

British soldiers onto his 21-person yacht. His role in the evacuation is dramatized by Mark Rylance in the 2017 movie *Dunkirk*.

unlikely to remote.* At 2 a.m. the surge to get on the few that remain grows so intense that the crew members have to lock arms to hold back the crowd. You aren't going to get a seat, which means you're going to have to swim. Fortunately, that isn't the death sentence it might seem. Lifeboats plucked at least five swimmers from the water and many more from two overturned lifeboats. With the proper preparation, you still have a chance.

When the *Titanic* band plays its final song—perhaps either "Songe d'Automne" or "Nearer, My God, to Thee" (eyewitness testimony is mixed)—that's your cue to head to the very stern of the boat. Move all the way to the back railing and hold on. *Titanic*'s bow will soon dip deep into the water, gradually lifting the stern so high its propellers clear the waterline. Once the boat gains approximately 20 degrees of tilt, it cracks in half. The bow drops to the bottom of the ocean, and the stern rises again.

As this happens, use your vantage point to look for the nearest lifeboats. According to the testimony of survivor Jack Thayer, most of the boats float some 400 to 500 yards away. Pick the nearest one, then locate and remember the stars above it. The lifeboat will be too far away and too low in the water to see once you're swimming, so you'll need some means of navigation. Before the final plunge, shed the fancy clothes, tighten your life jacket, and, if you have a warm hat, put it on.

As you hit the water you might worry the sinking boat will create a sucking vortex that would draw you into the depths—but survivors report no such thing. Joughin, who stayed on the boat until the end, later claimed his hair was never even mussed.

Still, your first moments in the frigid sea will be some of the most dangerous. The water is 27 degrees Fahrenheit—about as

---

*The ship carried four collapsible life rafts, too. Raft C left at 1:40 with 44 of 47 seats taken. Raft D left at 2:05 with 25 of 47 seats taken. The crew never launched rafts A and B, but they do float off *Titanic* as it sinks.

cold as any naturally occurring water on this planet. When you enter, you're going to experience a cold-shock response that causes a gasp even if your head is underwater. The inhale is uncontrollable—like your knee springing back to a doctor's reflex hammer—so replicating Joughin's entry is important. Keep your head above the water. Do not swan dive or jump. Instead, try to slip in. The freezing temperatures may also cause you to hyperventilate. Stay calm, slow your breathing, allow the life jacket to keep you afloat, and the shock should pass within sixty seconds. Then find your guiding star, and start swimming.

Swim at a pace you can maintain for ten to fifteen minutes, but work hard. The more heat you produce, the longer you'll stay alive. In this water, your body temperature will drop below 80 degrees after forty-five minutes, at which point you'll enter cardiac arrest. But in reality, you have far less time than that. A creeping numbness that begins on the tips of your toes and fingers will spread quickly. After only a few minutes your hands and feet will numb as blood retracts to your body's vital organs. After fifteen minutes, your arms and legs will numb to the point of incapacitation. At that point, without the life jacket, you would drown. You have one on, so you won't, but it will merely prolong the inevitable. No one will come to rescue you. You need to swim the entire 500 yards within the fifteen minutes that you'll have use of your arms and legs, or you'll bob about helplessly in your life jacket while you await cardiac arrest.

Nevertheless, 500 yards in fifteen minutes is manageable. At the International Ice Swimming Championships, the best usually swim that distance in fewer than seven. If you stay focused and don't become lost or entangled, you should make it.

The lifeboat should have plenty of open seats, as almost all were severely underfilled. But be careful as you climb out of the water. You may experience a dangerous decline in arterial blood pressure, particularly if you stand or exert yourself once aboard.

At least one *Titanic* swimmer died of a heart attack after a lifeboat pulled them from the water. Warm yourself as best you can, and wait for the rescue ship *Carpathia* that arrives at 4 a.m. Aboard the RMS *Carpathia*, you can uneventfully complete your voyage to New York City.

Once you arrive, pay a visit to the owner of the *Titanic*, Mr. J. P. Morgan himself. He lives at 219 Madison Avenue.

Ask for your £8 back.

HOW TO SURVIVE

THE WORST TORNADO IN AMERICAN HISTORY

Let's say you want to see a classic American rail town. Maybe you're a railfan. A train tourist. A "foamer," as conductors pejoratively call them. You want to see when rail tracks served as America's arteries, and when conductors in striped overalls powered American commerce.

So you travel back to March 18, 1925, to visit the train station in the small rail town of Gorham, Illinois. You'll watch as dozens of steam engines pull through one of the busiest crossings in America. You'll see soot-covered crews shovel coal into boilers. And at 2:30 that afternoon, you'll see a black fog approaching rapidly from the southwest.

At first, you may not be concerned. Like fog, this blackness has no discernable shape. There's no clear funnel curling down from a dark anvil cloud. There's no whip-like vortex framed against a clear sky. The dark mass merely blends into the towering cloud above, as if the cloud itself had merely sagged to the ground.

But concern may soon replace your initial curiosity when you notice the fog isn't behaving like a traditional watery gloom. As the seconds pass, you'll realize it's not creeping across the water or simply condensing across the horizon. It's ripping toward you like a stock car in fifth gear.

Then you'll hear its noise. What begins as a low hum will soon crescendo into a deafening shriek that one witness later describes as "a whistling, siren-like death song."

The "fog" you see is actually a sheath of heavy rain. Hiding behind it is the most powerful tornado in recorded history.

The "Tri-State Tornado," as the newspapers later dubbed it, was a meteorological freak. No tornado has ever blown harder, moved faster, or lasted longer. While the average tornado spins for fewer than ten minutes, Tri-State averaged 59 miles per hour over three and a half hours for 219 miles across three states. And while the average tornado advances at 30 miles per hour, when the Tri-State Tornado crossed the Mississippi River and smacked into Gorham, it was moving at an astonishing 73 miles per hour—the fastest in recorded history.

On the Enhanced Fujita scale, which meteorologists use to classify a tornado's power, a maximum EF 5 designation signifies sustained wind velocities of at least 200 miles per hour. Fewer than 1 percent of tornadoes even attain this speed. Tri-State dwarfed it. At its height, Tri-State's winds exceeded 300 miles per hour. Even among the rarest, most catastrophic weather events that can occur on earth, Tri-State stands above. It peeled pavement, unzipped railroad track, hurled hundred-ton locomotives, tossed tractors into homes, and splintered nearly every building it touched. It cut a mile-wide gash through southern Missouri, Illinois, and Indiana, and killed at least 695 people—double the death toll of the second deadliest tornado in American history.

The Tri-State Tornado holds every significant tornadic record that a twisted cloud could ever hope to accomplish. It's the Secretariat of tornadoes, and southwestern Illinois was the backstretch of its Belmont. If young clouds hung posters on their wall, they would be shots of the Tri-State supercell as it crossed the Mississippi. There may not be, in the recorded history of atmospheric wrath, a single more ominous sight than the shrieking black fog you see from the window of the Gorham train station at 2:30 that March afternoon.

The Tri-State Tornado's demonic combination of speed, duration, and power make it such a meteorological anomaly that almost a century later a group of tornado experts led by Robert Maddox, the former director of the National Severe Storms Laboratory, set out to discover how the skies produced such a monster. According to Maddox, it began, as nearly all weather systems do, with a drop in pressure.

Tornadoes are the end result of an extraordinary series of events involving so many variables that many meteorologists doubt whether we will ever be able to predict their formation with any certainty. At their core, though, they are the explosive, unpredictable result of an atmospheric contortionist act that occurs when air masses of different temperatures and humidities collide.

Smaller versions of these collisions occur every day all over the globe, but the North American Midwest hosts more than 75 percent of the world's tornadoes because its long flatlands provide a unique, unobstructed atmospheric pathway from Mexico to Canada. As a result, collisions in the Midwest play out on a continental scale. Every spring, when the winter jet stream still blows with enough force to create a strong low-pressure vacuum, and when the skies above Mexico warm but it remains cold over Canada, the Midwest hosts the atmosphere's greatest demolition derby. And because low pressure draws air in, its development acts like the carny's opening call.

At 7 p.m. on March 16, 1925, two days before your arrival in Illinois, jet stream winds blasting west to east above Helena, Montana, swerved into the lee of the Rocky Mountains. This sudden, southerly swing created an atmospheric vacuum—called a "low pressure trough"—above western Montana. The vacuum sucked in hot, dry air from the deserts of Mexico; cool, moist air from the Gulf; and frigid air from over the southern Canadian tundra. The triumvirate of airs moved toward low pressure, but areas of low pressure are not stationary targets. They move down the jet stream like the undulation in a flicked rope, so that eighteen hours after the low pressure's initial formation it no longer sat over Helena, but had moved almost 1,500 miles to the south-southwest. On the morning of March 17, Mexican desert air and muggy Gulf air finally caught up and impacted above Springfield, Missouri.

When hot, dry desert air collides with the cool, moist air from the Mexican Gulf, the two blocks of air don't blend together; they slam and slide like the scrum in a rugby match. The change in wind, temperature, and humidity can occur so suddenly that someone crossing the street could feel the shift in weather in the time it takes to reach the far side. This vertical line of impact—called a "dry line"—begins at the ground and rises tens of thousands of feet into the high atmosphere, but as it does, it doesn't remain perfectly perpendicular. Instead, shifting winds above the ground can push the hot, dry, Mexican desert air over cool, moist air from the Gulf. This arrangement—called a "cap"—is an atmospheric pipe bomb.

Normally, hot air sits below cool. But in the twisted pileup of this collision, the temperature actually warms as it gains altitude. The result is potentially explosive. As the day warms, ground-hugging air warmed by the radiant heat of the earth cannot rise. Instead it sits, its temperature climbs, and the pressure beneath the cap builds like a boiling kettle with no spout. Storm chasers call this situation the loaded gun. But for the gun to go off, there must be a trigger. Something must lift the Gulf air above the thin, hot cap. In the most powerful storms, that trigger is wind.

By lunchtime on March 18, the cold air and southerly winds from Canada finally arrived and smashed into the Gulf's northerly gusts. Like two speeding jalopies, the two opposing winds impacted and lifted in the collision, boosting the wet Gulf air through the cap. In the cooler air of the upper atmosphere, the warm, wet air rocketed upward at speeds in excess of 70 miles per hour.

Finally, after rising as high as 60,000 feet, the updraft lost its heat, dumped its water to form clouds and rain, and lost even more heat in the chemical conversion. Now supercooled and dense, the air plummeted back down, smashing into the earth and ejecting outward with enough force to cause tornado-like damage on the ground.

Like opposing currents twisting into a river's vortex, the winds in the cloud began to rotate around each other. The result was a spinning-saucer-like thundercloud with an eerie turquoise glow— a product of the sun filtering through rain and ice—called a supercell.

Most supercells do not form tornadoes. They deliver baseball-sized hail, lightning, thunder, torrential rain, and powerful winds, and though they twist menacingly, few ever bring that rotation to earth. But if the updraft and downdraft blasting into and around the thundercloud along the ground pinch together, they can begin to twist around each other. And if the supercell's updraft is strong enough, it can lift and stretch this horizontal vortex into its cloud—a process that greatly increases the wind's rotation for the same reason an ice skater's spin rate increases when the skater pulls in their arms. In seconds, an updraft can tighten a large, circuitous rotation capable of banging a house's screen door into a tube of focused fury that can rip a house from its foundation.

At 1:01 p.m. on March 18, 1925, three miles outside Ellington, Missouri, the winds of the Tri-State supercell crossed this threshold.

According to witnesses, the tornado began both narrow and elongate in the classic and easily identifiable tornadic formation, but within minutes the small twisting tornado grew to more than a mile in diameter. Soon afterward, a forty-nine-year-old farmer named Samuel Flowers became its first victim when he was overtaken just outside Ellington while trying to escape on horseback.

Sitting in the train station in Gorham, Illinois, you're nearly one hundred miles from Mr. Flowers. Ordinarily, that would place you comfortably out of a tornado's range. Normally, nature cannot sustain the cohesion required to maintain a tornado for longer than a few miles, and long before it arrived in Gorham it would have run out of pressurized air or wandered away from the area of the tornado-forming collision.

But that's not what happened. This time, sitting in the Gorham's train station not only places you comfortably within this tornado's range; it places you in the exact location where it will reach its greatest fury.

The meteorological explanation for Tri-State's unprecedented stamina begins with an entirely unrelated rain squall that happened to pass through earlier that morning. The rain chilled the air over southern Illinois and created a large temperature difference over a small area. Because tornadoes feed off both warm and cool air, the rain shower laid what amounted to a narrow, tornado-friendly track across the Midwest. And in an unprecedented display of cohesion, the supercell, the dry line, and the low-pressure system all moved in unison straight down the narrow band like a blindfolded motorcyclist blasting down a tightrope.

PATH OF THE TRI-STATE TORNADO

MORNING OF MARCH 18, 1925

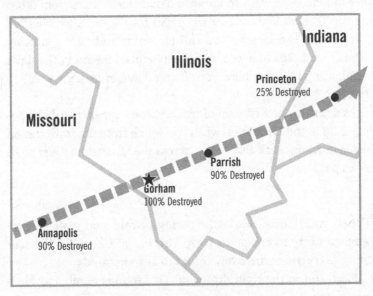

Indiana

Illinois

Princeton
25% Destroyed

Missouri

Parrish
90% Destroyed

Gorham
100% Destroyed

Annapolis
90% Destroyed

In the 1920s the Midwest had no tornado warning system. This was partially on purpose, as back then a tornado forecast never reliably produced anything more than panic. The U.S. Weather Bureau even went so far as to ban its forecasters from uttering the T-word. If you check the paper for the day's weather, all you'll see in the forecast is a call for "rains and strong shifting winds"—a 1920s meteorological euphemism meaning the day's weather might either blow your house down or be a good day to fly a kite.

As a result, the first sign of trouble won't appear until just before 2:30 in the afternoon, when you watch from the train station as the howling black cloud tears across the Mississippi River at 70 miles per hour.

When you realize the terror racing toward you, you may be tempted to try to escape its path. This is a mistake. But if you're going to try, there are a few things to keep in mind.

First, run in the right direction. This sounds dumb and obvious. It isn't.

Instinct may compel you to run in the opposite direction of the tornado's approach. This is wrong. The tornado is advancing at the pace of a speeding train. Running away from it would be like escaping a train by running down the tracks. Pursue this path and you will, at best, delay your demise by a few seconds.

Instead, you should run perpendicular to its path. In this case, as in the case of most tornadoes (but not all!), you need to run north or south. Like most tornadoes, Tri-State tracks east-northeast as it follows the path of the jet stream. Clearing the path of the tornado would be fairly simple in ideal conditions. Even the comparatively massive vortex of the Tri-State only spans a mile in width, which means you could escape if you move just a half mile. If you're a strong runner performing in ideal conditions, you could cover the distance in five or so minutes. Unfortunately, conditions are far from perfect. And it's not just the buckets of rain and baseball-sized hail. The real killer is the headwind.

As a tornado advances, it draws air into its updraft like a superpowered vacuum, creating a hellacious headwind preceding its path. The colliding fronts to its north and south compound the problem. These blow wind from both north and south into the inflow, placing you in a pincer-movement-like vice of jet-exhaust-level headwinds. This deeply complicates the running conditions for a bipedal creature like yourself.

Humans, with our broad chests, are almost uniquely ill-suited to move into the wind. Evolution has finely tuned our bodies into near-perfect pendulums. Our weight is aligned over our hips so that we can gently tip over, catch our fall, and repeat the process—aka walk—in a remarkably efficient way. Headwinds ruin all of that. Our broad, flat, rectangular chests turn into sails. In 70-mile-per-hour winds, you need to lean forward 15 degrees just to stand upright. Running into them is like sprinting up a 25-degree slope. You'll watch as dogs, deer, and most of the ambulatory animal kingdom use their sleek, aerodynamic bodies to cut through the wind while you'll likely end up hanging on to a lamppost and cursing your sail of a chest.

You could instead attempt to drive away, but again, the wind may foil your escape. In 1925, one of the most popular cars in America was the 20-horsepower Ford Model T. According to the manual, the Model T tops out at 45 miles per hour. Not bad, but there's a catch. The aerodynamics of the car are so poor that *Road & Track* likens it to a barn door. That's a problem in 100-mile-per-hour headwinds. Combine that with an inefficient engine and gearing issues that reduce horsepower at low velocity, and you have a car that, by my math, will redline at a speed only barely outpacing a runner.* To make matters worse, the cabin of a Model T might be the worst tornado shelter in the history of human engineering. You'll be stuck inside a car with no safety features of any kind save for the horn. It has no seat belts, no airbags, a large plate-glass window, and aerodynamics that make it a serviceable kite in high winds. In the nearby city of Murphysboro, Illinois, the Tri-State Tornado will launch a Model T over a building. Don't be in that car. Or any car. Or even try to escape. Instead, you need to hide.

When I ask Maddox whether it's safer for you to run or drive away from the Tri-State Tornado, he advises neither. "Seeking shelter is wiser," he says. Instead of running or driving, he advises you to use what little time you have to hunker down behind as many walls as possible, and then wait as the most powerful winds in recorded history approach.

That doesn't mean you should stay where you are. Some buildings are safer than others, and the train station happens to perform particularly poorly. The tornado hurls more than a dozen boxcars parked along the tracks, some into the railway station itself. Nothing remains of the wooden structure but the foundation. You may not be able to escape the tornado, but you do at least need to leave.

Unfortunately, not a single building in Gorham survives the tornado intact. Because the entire town fit inside the girth of the storm, it's one of the few cities in history to sustain 100 percent tornadic destruction. So there are no great options, but there are particularly bad ones. Even within a tornado, there are mini-vortices of intense wind speed—small tornadoes within the

---

*If anything, I suspect 10 miles per hour might be a little optimistic. If you consider the reduced traction generated by the wind's lift (Model T's do not have spoilers) and that the engine's gearing would not allow it to produce peak power at such low speeds, I think you might find yourself keeping pace with the runners.

tornado itself that inflict catastrophic damage. These mini-vortices explain why one house might be lifted from its foundation while its neighbor merely loses its roof. In Gorham, Tri-State focuses its fury over Main Street, where vortices completely demolish the two-story bank, implode the town's large school, fling its multiton railway cars, and destroy its train station.

Instead of running away from the tornado, use your three minutes to run south-southwest, *toward* the oncoming tornado. That may seem like a dangerous choice, but Park Street is just two blocks to your southwest, and some of the houses on this street escape with far less damage than those on Main.

The shield of heavy rain will have passed over you by the time you reach Park Street, and if you look up you may now be able to see the focus of the storm. You may see a massive black cone descending from an even larger black anvil cloud, rotating and rising high above the cruising altitude of passenger jets. The twisting descent of the tornado likely won't resemble the traditional, defined, photogenic, whip-like ones more frequently photographed. It's too wide, too powerful, and has picked up too much debris for that. Instead, it may seem as if the cloud itself has merely sagged to the ground. This development only makes the storm more dangerous. It obfuscates the speed and location of its twisting winds and makes it far more difficult to determine the tornado's true outline.

But you shouldn't pay any attention to that. Instead, as you sprint down Park, you need to check the names on mailboxes. According to a newspaper account published in *The Daily Independent* a few days after the storm, only a handful of houses escaped total destruction in Gorham, and one of them was owned by a Mr. T. L. Spillman. According to this account, his house even served as a shelter for the wounded after the storm passed. So it should survive. Just don't stay with his neighbor. The same article says that house was flattened.

Once inside, grab the strongest, largest pot you can find from the kitchen—you'll need this in a second. Then find the lowest, smallest room in the house and stuff yourself inside. A closet, a room under the stairs, or a bathtub provides a decent tornado shelter in the absence of a real one. A basement or an actual underground shelter would be ideal, but midwestern townships primarily built their shelters in response to the Tri-State storm, not before it. So a small room with sturdy walls to protect you from the hail of debris is essential. Once you're safely stowed away, take the large pot and put it on your head. You're going to use it as a helmet.

Small rooms and stewpots are both good ideas because the primary danger in a tornado is not the strong winds themselves, but what those winds throw. The Tri-State Tornado will hurl cars, tractors, trains, and in one case will drive a wood plank sixteen inches into a tree. As the tornado passes over you, thousands of splinters, nails, two-by-fours, and train cars will fill the air, and every solid wall, bathtub, or stewpot you can place between yourself and those millions of projectiles might make the difference. Ideally, you would be underground while the chaos swarms above. But in your desperate situation, Mr. Spillman's iron pot and closet will have to do. Close yourself inside and wait as the roar of the wind crescendos into a howling scream periodically punctuated by the sounds of crashing boxcars, tractors, cars, and the splintering of houses. If you look up, and if you can see into the tornado's cone, you'll see flashes of lightning illuminate the dark twister, silhouetting bits of houses, railroad tracks, spikes, tractors, cars, and entire trees, all spinning within or ejected from the howling vortex.

Fortunately, the horror passes in moments. Traveling at 70 miles per hour, the tornado will rip through Gorham in less than a minute. With a quick northwestern sweep, the supercell will flatten the town before advancing through the rest of southern Illinois and on to Indiana.

Of Gorham's five hundred residents, more than half suffer injuries and at least thirty-four people perish. There may not be, in the entirety of America's long tornadic history, a worse place to be than in Gorham, Illinois, at 2:35 p.m. on the afternoon of March 18, 1925. That may make it a dangerous place to see a steam locomotive, but it is one of the only places and times in history when you can see one of the hundred-ton machines take flight.

ACKNOWLEDGMENTS

This book could not have been possible without the incredible generosity of an amazing array of creative and talented people who provided me with their unending patience, guidance, ideas, research, and time. A complete list of all those whose work helped bring this book to fruition would be impossible to list in this space, but a few served such critical roles they deserve particular thanks.

Thank you to my Dad, for always being my first reader. Thank you to Isabella Jibilian, for her dogged research and boundless enthusiasm. Thank you to Sarah Fallon, for her early thoughts that proved so formative to this book's direction. Thank you to Kevin Plottner, for turning my garbled visions into wonderfully clear, gloriously gruesome illustrations. Thank you to Alia Habib, for her incredible guidance and ceaseless support. Thank you to Annika Karody and the entire Penguin team for their wise edits, gorgeous design, and countless tasks required to bring this book into the world. And thank you to my editor, Meg Leder, for her brilliant assistance at every stage.

RESOURCES AND FURTHER READING

THE DINOSAUR AGE

Alexander, R. McNeill. "How Dinosaurs Ran." *Scientific American* 264, no. 4 (April 1991): 130–37.

Black, Riley. "What Did Dinosaurs Smell Like?" *Scientific American, Laelaps* (blog), January 8, 2020.

DePalma, Robert A., et al. "The First Giant Raptor (Theropoda: Dromaeosauridae) from the Hell Creek Formation." *Paleontological Contributions* 14 (October 30, 2015): 1–16.

DiMatteo, Steve. "An Interview with Thomas R. Holtz, Dinosaur Rock Star." RobotButt.com, June 12, 2015.

Fitzgerald, Richard. "How Fast Could *Tyrannosaurus rex* Run?" *Physics Today* 55, no. 4 (2002): 18.

Graham, Kathy. "Could Dinosaurs Climb?" *ABC Science,* April 18, 2012.

Haldane, J. B. S. "On Being the Right Size." *Harper's Magazine,* March 1926.

Hirt, Myriam, et al. "A General Scaling Law Reveals Why the Largest Animals Are Not the Fastest." *Nature Ecology & Evolution* 1 (July 2017): 1116–22.

Hutchinson, John, and Mariano Garcia. "*Tyrannosaurus* Was Not a Fast Runner." *Nature* 415 (2002): 1018–21.

Levy, Dawn. "Speedy Elephants Use a Biomechanical Trick to 'Run' like Groucho." Press release. *Stanford News Service,* March 31, 2003.

O'Luanaigh, Cian. "First Evidence That Some Dinosaurs Were Nocturnal." *New Scientist*, April 14, 2001.

Pontzer, Herman, et al. "Biomechanics of Running Indicates Endothermy in Bipedal Dinosaurs." *Plos One* 4, no. 11 (November 2009): e7783.

Sellers, William I. "March of the Titans: The Locomotor Capabilities of Sauropod Dinosaurs." *Plos One* 8, no. 10 (October 2013): e78733.

Sellers, William I., and Phillip L. Manning. "Estimating Dinosaur Maximum Running Speeds Using Evolutionary Robotics." *Proceedings of the Royal Society B: Biological Sciences* 274, no. 1626 (2007): 2711–16.

Sellers, William I., et al. "Investigating the Running Abilities of *Tyrannosaurus* rex Using Stress-Constrained Multibody Dynamic Analysis." *PeerJ* 5 (2017): e3420.

Snively, Eric., et al. "Lower Rotational Inertia and Larger Leg Muscles Indicate More Rapid Turns in Tyrannosaurids Than in Other Large Theropods." *PeerJ* 7 (2019): e6432.

Wilson, Alan M. "Biomechanics of Predator-Prey Arms Race in Lion, Zebra, Cheetah and Impala." *Nature* 554 (January 2018): 183–88.

THE CHICXULUB ASTEROID

Amos, Jonathan. "Dinosaur Asteroid Hit 'Worst Possible Place.'" *BBC Science*, May 15, 2017.

Bardeen, Charles G., et al. "On Transient Climate Change at the Cretaceous-Paleogene Boundary Due to Atmospheric Soot Injections." *Proceedings of the National Academy of Science* 114, no. 36 (2017): e7415—e7424.

Chesley, Steven R., and Steven N. Ward. "A Quantitative Assessment of the Human and Economic Hazard from Impact-Generated Tsunami." *Natural Hazards* 38 (2006): 355–74.

Collins, G. S., et al. "A Steeply-Inclined Trajectory for the Chicxulub Impact." *Nature Communications* 11 (2020): 1480.

French, Bevan M. *Traces of Catastrophe: A Handbook of Shock-Metamorphic Effects in Terrestrial Meteorite Impact Structures*. Houston: Lunar and Planetary Institute, 1998. LPI Contribution No. 954.

Kaiho, Kunio, and Naga Oshima. "Site of Asteroid Impact Changed the History of Life on Earth: The Low Probability of Mass Extinction." *Scientific Reports* 7 (2017): 14855.

Labandeira, Conrad C., et al. "Preliminary Assessment of Insect Herbivory Across the Cretaceous-Tertiary Boundary: Major Extinction and Minimum Rebound." In *The Hell Creek Formation of the Northern Great Plains*, edited by Joseph H. Hartman et al., 297–327. Boulder, CO: Geological Society of America, 2002. Special Paper 361.

Lyzenga, Gregory A. "Why Are Impact Craters Always Round?" *Scientific American*, October 21, 1999.

Motiwala, Samira., et al. "An Integrated Physics-Based Risk Model for Assessing the Asteroid Threat." NASA Technical Reports (2015): 464–72.

Preston, Douglas. "The Day the Dinosaurs Died." *The New Yorker*, April 8, 2019.

Register, Paul J., et al. "Asteroid Fragmentation Approaches for Modeling Atmospheric Energy Deposition." *Icarus* 284 (March 2017): 157–66.

Renne, Paul R., et al. "Time Scales of Critical Events Around the Cretaceous-Paleogene Boundary." *Science* 339, no. 6120 (February 8, 2013): 684–87.

Sanders, Robert. "66-Million-Year-Old Deathbed Linked to Dinosaur-Killing Meteor." *Berkeley Research*, March 29, 2019.

Shonting, David, and Cathy Ezrailson. *Chicxulub: The Impact and Tsunami*. Switzerland: Springer International, 2017.

Stephens, Tim. "Reign of the Giant Insects Ended with the Evolution of Birds." *UC Santa Cruz Magazine*, June 4, 2012.

THE ICE AGE

Agam, Aviad, and Ran Barkai. "Elephant and Mammoth Hunting During the Paleolithic: A Review of the Relevant Archaeological, Ethnographic and Ethno-Historical Records." *Quaternary* 1, no. 1 (2018): 3.

Arbic, Brian K., et al. "Ocean Tides and Heinrich Events." *Nature* 432 (2004): 460.

Bell, W. D. M. "Wanderings of an Elephant Hunter." *Country Life* (London), 1923.

Buis, Alan. "Milankovitch (Orbital) Cycles and Their Role in Earth's Climate." *NASA News*, February 27, 2020.

Coogan, Joe. "Hunting Africa's Most Dangerous Game." *Sporting Classics Daily*, June 9, 2021.

Demay, Laëtitia, et al. "Utilization of Mammoth Resources and Occupation of the Dniester-Prut Basin Territory: The Upper Palaeolithic Site of Valea Morilor (Republic of Moldova)." *Quaternary Science Reviews* 222 (October 15, 2019).

Gavashelishvili, Alexander, and David Tarkhnishvili. "Biomes and Human Distribution During the Last Ice Age." *Global Ecology and Biogeography* 25, no. 5 (2016): 563–74.

Guthrie, R. Dale. "Origin and Causes of the Mammoth Steppe: A Story of Cloud Cover, Woolly Mammal Tooth Pits, Buckles, and Inside-Out Beringia." *Quaternary Science Reviews* 20 (2001): 549–74.

Macdonald, Francis A., et al. "Arc-Continent Collisions in the Tropics Set Earth's Climate State." *Science* 364, no. 6436 (March 2019): 181–84.

Tallavaara, Miikka, et al. "Human Population Dynamics in Europe over the Last Glacial Maximum." *PNAS* 112, no. 27 (June 22, 2015): 8232–37.

Tierney, Jessica E., et al. "Glacial Cooling and Climate Sensitivity Revisited." *Nature* 584 (2020): 569–73.

Whittaker, John. "Atlatls Are Levers, Not Springs." *Bulletin of Primitive Technology* 48 (Fall 2014): 68–73.

Wojtal, Piotr, et al. "Carnivores in the Everyday Life of Gravettian Hunters-Gatherers in Central Europe." *Journal of Anthropological Archaeology* 59 (September 2020): 101171.

Wojtal, Piotr, et al. "The Earliest Direct Evidence of Mammoth Hunting in Central Europe—The Kraków Spadzista Site (Poland)." *Quaternary Science Reviews* 213 (June 2019): 162–66.

Zdziebłowski, Szymon. "The First Evidence in Europe That Man Was Hunting Mammoths Discovered." *Science in Poland,* July 1, 2019.

ANCIENT EGYPT

Arnold, Dieter. *Building in Egypt: Pharaonic Stone Masonry.* Oxford: Oxford University Press, 1991.

Blanchard, W. O. "Father Nile and Egyptian Agriculture." *The Scientific Monthly,* March 1937.

Brier, Bob. "The History of Ancient Egypt: The Great Lectures by Bob Brier." The *Great Courses,* 1999.

Brier, Bob, and Hoyt Hobbs. *Daily Life of the Ancient Egyptians.* Westwood, CT: Greenwood, 1999.

"Briton Falls to His Death After Dozing Off atop Pyramid." Associated Press, April 24, 1989.

"Excavating the Lost City." *NOVA*, PBS, December 31, 2009.

Fall, A., et al. "Sliding Friction on Wet and Dry Sand." *Physical Review Letters 112* (2014): 175502.

Filer, Joyce. "Health Hazards and Cures in Ancient Egypt." BBC, February, 17, 2011.

Fowlie, Tom. "Decoding the Great Pyramid." *NOVA*, PBS, April 30, 2019.

Hawass, Zahi. "The Discovery of the Tombs of the Pyramid Builders at Giza." Guardians.net, 1997, www.guardians.net/hawass/build tomb.htm.

Hawass, Zahi. *Mountains of the Pharaohs: The Untold Stories of the Pyramid Builders*. New York: Doubleday, 2006.

Jackson, Kevin, and Jonathan Stamp. *Building the Great Pyramid*. Ontario, Canada: Firefly Books, 2003.

Lehner, Mark. *The Complete Pyramids: Solving the Ancient Mysteries*. London: Thames & Hudson, 1997.

Lehner, Mark, and Zahi Hawass. *Giza and the Pyramids: The Definitive History*. Chicago: University of Chicago Press, 2017.

Mertz, Barbara. *Red Land, Black Land: Daily Life in Ancient Egypt*. New York: Dodd, Mead, 1978.

Monnier, Franck, and Alexander Puchkov. "The Construction Phases of the Bent Pyramid at Dahshur: A Reassessment." *ENiM* 9 (2016): 15–36.

Moores, Bob. *Building the Pyramids: How Did They Do It?* Bloomington, IN: iUniverse, 2019.

Shaw, Jonathan. "Who Built the Pyramids?" *Harvard Magazine*, July–August 2003.

"Two Boy Scouts Killed in Tug-of-War Accident." Associated Press, June 6, 1995.

POMPEII

Acocella, Joan. "The Terror and the Fascination of Pompeii." *The New Yorker*, February 10, 2020.

Di Renzo, V., et al. "Magmatic History of Somma-Vesuvius on the Basis of New Geochemical and Isotopic Data from a Deep Borehole

(Camaldoli della Torre)." *Journal of Petrology* 48, no. 4 (April 2007): 753–84.

Geggel, Laura. "Mount Vesuvius Didn't Kill Everyone in Pompeii. Where Did the Survivors Go?" *LiveScience,* February 26, 2019.

Huff, W. D., and L. A. Owen. "Volcanic Landforms and Hazards." *Treatise on Geomorphology 5* (2015): 148–92.

Lima, Annamaria, et al. "Influence of Hydrothermal Processes on Geochemical Variations Between 79 AD and 1944 AD Vesuvius Eruptions." *Developments in Volcanology* 9 (2006): 235–47.

Mastrolorenzo, Giuseppe, et al. "Herculaneum Victims of Vesuvius in AD 79." *Nature* 410 (April 12, 2001): 769–70.

Paone, Angelo. "The Geochemical Evolution of the Mt. Somma–Vesuvius Volcano." *Mineralogy and Petrology* 87 (May 2006): 53–80.

Petrone, Pierpaolo, et al. "Heat-Induced Brain Vitrification from the Vesuvius Eruption in C.E. 79." *New England Journal of Medicine* 382 (2020): 383–84.

Rosenbaum, Gideon, et al. "Kinematics of Slab Tear Faults During Subduction Segmentation and Implications for Italian Magmatism." *Tectonics* 27, no. 2 (April 2008).

Scandone, Roberto, et al. "Death, Survival and Damage During the 79 AD Eruption of Vesuvius Which Destroyed Pompeii and Herculaneum." *J-Reading: Journal of Research and Didactics in Geography 2* (December 2019).

Scarth, Alwyn, and Jean-Claude Tanguy. *Volcanoes of Europe.* Oxford: Oxford University Press, 2001.

THE SACK OF ROME

Beard, Mary. *SPQR: A History of Ancient Rome.* New York: Liveright, 2015.

Boin, Douglas. *Alaric the Goth: An Outsider's History of the Fall of Rome.* New York: W. W. Norton, 2020.

Burns, Thomas S. *Barbarians Within the Gates of Rome: A Study of Roman Military Policy and the Barbarians, ca. 375–425 A.D.* Bloomington: Indiana University Press, 1995.

Delorme, Charles D., Jr., et al. "Rent Seeking and Taxation in the Ancient Roman Empire." *Applied Economics* 37, no. 6 (2005): 705–11.

Erdkamp, Paul. "Soldiers, Roman Citizens, and Latin Colonists in Mid-Republican Italy." *Ancient Society* 41 (2011): 109–46.

Gibbon, Edward. *The History of the Decline and Fall of the Roman Empire.* 6 *vols.* London: Strahan & Cadell, 1776–1789.

Godden, M. R. "The Anglo-Saxons and the Goths: Rewriting the Sack of Rome." *Anglo-Saxon England* 31 (2002): 47–68.

Heather, Peter. *The Fall of the Roman Empire: A New History of Rome and the Barbarians.* Oxford: Oxford University Press, 2006.

Kirsch, Adam. "The Empire Strikes Back." *The New Yorker,* January 1, 2012.

Kulikowski, Michael. *The Tragedy of Empire: From Constantine to the Destruction of Roman Italy.* Boston: Belknap, 2019.

Mathisen, Ralph. "Barbarian Invasions or Civil Wars: Goths as Auxiliary Forces in the Roman Army." In *Empire in Crisis: Gothic Invasions and Roman Historiography,* edited by Fritz Mitthof et al., 263–88. Vienna: Holzhausen, 2020.

Retief, Francois P., and Louise Cilliers. "Causes of Death Among the Caesars (27 BC–AD 476)." *Acta Theologica* 26, no. 2, (2006): Supplement 7.

Tan, James. *Power and Public Finance at Rome, 264–49 BCE.* Oxford: Oxford University Press, 2017.

THE DARKEST YEAR OF THE DARK AGES

Arjava, Antti. "The Mystery Cloud of 536 CE in the Mediterranean Sources." *Dumbarton Oaks Papers* 59 (2005): 73–94.

Cahill, Thomas. *How the Irish Saved Civilization.* New York: Doubleday, 1995.

Downham, Clare. *Medieval Ireland.* Cambridge: Cambridge University Press, 2018.

Gunn, Joel, and Alessio Ciarini. *The AD 536 Crisis: A 21st-Century Perspective.* Campeche, Mexico: Universidad Autónoma de Campeche, 2021. Series: Información 18.

Helama, Samuli, et al. "Volcanic Dust Veils from Sixth Century Tree-Ring Isotopes Linked to Reduced Irradiance, Primary Production and Human Health." *Scientific Reports* 8 (2018): 1339.

Higham, Nicholas. *King Arthur: The Making of the Legend.* New Haven: Yale University Press, 2018.

Hindley, Geoffrey. *A Brief History of the Anglo-Saxons*. London: Robinson, 2006.

Jordan, William C. *The Great Famine: Northern Europe in the Early Fourteenth Century*. Princeton: Princeton University Press, 1996.

Keys, David. *Catastrophe: An Investigation into the Origins of the Modern World*. New York: Ballantine, 1999.

McCormick, Michael. *Origins of the European Economy: Communications and Commerce AD 300–900*. Cambridge: Cambridge University Press, 2001.

McCormick, Michael, et al. "Climate Change During and After the Roman Empire: Reconstructing the Past from Scientific and Historical Evidence." *Journal of Interdisciplinary History* 43, no. 2 (2012): 169–220.

Newfield, Timothy P. "The Climate Downturn of 536–50." In *The Palgrave Handbook of Climate History*, edited by Sam White et al., 447–93. London: Palgrave Macmillan, 2018.

Sigl, M., et al. "Timing and Climate Forcing of Volcanic Eruptions for the Past 2,500 Years." *Nature* 523 (2015): 543–49.

Stenseth, Nils Chr., et al. "Plague Dynamics Are Driven by Climate Variation." *PNAS* 103, no. 35 (2006): 13110–115.

Tepper, Alexander, and Karol Jan Borowiecki. "Accounting for Breakout in Britain: The Industrial Revolution Through a Malthusian Lens." *Federal Reserve Bank of New York Staff Reports* (September 2013): No. 639.

Zielinski, Sarah. "Plague Pandemic May Have Been Driven by Climate, Not Rats." *Smithsonian*, February 23, 2015.

THE BLACK DEATH

Anand, Mulk Raj. *Letters on India*. London: George Routledge & Sons, 1942.

Benedictow, Ole J. *The Black Death, 1346–1353: The Complete History*. London: BCA, 2004.

Christakos, George, et al. *Interdisciplinary Public Health Reasoning and Epidemic Modelling: The Case of Black Death*. New York: Springer, 2005.

Defoe, Daniel. *A Journal of the Plague Year*. London: E. Nutt, J. Roberts, A. Dodd, J. Graves, 1722.

Demeure, Christian E. "*Yersinia pestis* and Plague: An Updated View on Evolution, Virulence Determinants, Immune Subversion, Vaccination, and Diagnostics." *Genes & Immunity* 20, no. 5 (2019): 357–70.

DeWitte, Sharon N. "Age Patterns of Mortality During the Black Death in London, A.D. 1349–1350." *Journal of Archaeological Science* 37, no. 12 (2010): 3394–3400.

Eisner, Manuel. "Interactive London Medieval Murder Map." Cambridge: University of Cambridge, Institute of Criminology, 2018.

Eroshenko, Galina A., et al. "*Yersinia pestis* Strains of Ancient Phylogenetic Branch 0.ANT Are Widely Spread in the High-Mountain Plague Foci of Kyrgyzstan." *PLoS One* 12, no. 10 (2017): e0187230.

Green, Monica H., ed. *Pandemic Disease in the Medieval World: Rethinking the Black Death*. Kalamazoo, MI/Bradford, UK: ARC Medieval Press, 2014. Series: The Medieval Globe, vol. 1.

Ibeji, Mike. "Black Death." BBC, March 10, 2011.

Kendall, E. J., et al. "Mobility, Mortality, and the Middle Ages: Identification of Migrant Individuals in a 14th-Century Black Death Cemetery Population." *American Journal of Physical Anthropology* 150, no. 2 (2013): 210–22.

Koyama, Mark, et al. "Pandemics, Places, and Populations: Evidence from the Black Death." Centre for Economic Policy Research, Discussion Paper DP13523, February 12, 2019.

McNeill, William H. *Plagues and Peoples*. New York: Anchor, 1976.

Meek, James. "In 1348." *London Review of Books* 42, no. 7 (April 2, 2020).

Mortimer, Ian. *The Time Traveler's Guide to Medieval England: A Handbook for Visitors to the Fourteenth Century*. New York: Touchstone, 2011.

Walløe, Lars. "Medieval and Modern Bubonic Plague: Some Clinical Continuities." *Medical History* 52, Supplement 27 (2008): 59–73.

Wessely, Simon. "A Plague on All Your Houses." *The Guardian*, August 13, 2004.

Zhou, Dongsheng, et al. "Molecular and Physiological Insights into Plague Transmission, Virulence and Etiology." *Microbes and Infection* 8, no. 1 (January 2006): 273–84.

THE FALL OF CONSTANTINOPLE

Hankins, J. "Renaissance Crusaders: Humanist Crusade Literature in the Age of Mehmed II." *Dumbarton Oaks Papers* 49 (1995): 111–207.

King, Ross. *The Bookseller of Florence: The Story of the Manuscripts That Illuminated the Renaissance.* New York: Grove Atlantic, 2021.

Kraye, Jill. "The Revival of Hellenistic Philosophies." In *The Cambridge Companion to Renaissance Philosophy,* edited by James Hankins, 97–112. Cambridge: Cambridge University Press, 2007.

Laiou, Angeliki E., and Cécile Morrisson. *The Byzantine Economy.* Cambridge: Cambridge University Press, 2007.

Nedelcu, Silviu-Constantin. "The Libraries in the Byzantine Empire (330–1453)." *Annals of the University of Craiova for Journalism, Communication and Management* 2 (2016): 74–92.

Philippides, Marios, and Walter K. Hanak. *The Siege and the Fall of Constantinople in 1453: Historiography, Topography, and Military Studies.* London: Routledge, 2011.

Wickham, Chris. *Medieval Europe.* New Haven: Yale University Press, 2016.

THE FIRST CIRCUMNAVIGATION

Bergreen, Laurence. *Over the Edge of the World: Magellan's Terrifying Circumnavigation of the Globe.* Boston: Mariner, 2003.

Blane, Gilbert. *Observations on the Diseases Incident to Seamen.* London: Cooper, 1785.

Milne, Iain. "Who Was James Lind, and What Exactly Did He Achieve." *Journal of the Royal Society of Medicine* 105, no. 12 (December 2012): 503–508.

Penn-Barwell, Jowan G. "Sir Gilbert Blane FRS: The Man and His Legacy." *Journal of the Royal Naval Medical Service* 102 (2016): 61–66.

Pigafetta, Antonio. *Journal of Magellan's voyage,* ca. 1525.

Price, Catherine. "The Age of Scurvy." *Science History Institute,* August 14, 2017.

Weschler, Lawrence. "Comment." *The New Yorker,* November 1, 1987, www.newyorker.com/magazine/1987/11/09/comment-6308.

White, Marcus. "James Lind. The Man Who Helped to Cure Scurvy Lemons." *BBC News,* October 4, 2016.

Zweig, Stefan. *Conqueror of the Seas: The Story of Magellan.* Translated by Eden and Cedar Paul. New York: Viking, 1938. Ebook: *Magellan: Conqueror of the Seas.* Lexington, MA: Plunkett Lake Press, 2016.

A VOYAGE WITH BLACKBEARD

Crain, Caleb. "Bootylicious." *The New Yorker,* September 7, 2009.

Johnson, Steven. *Enemy of All Mankind: A True Story of Piracy, Power, and History's First Global Manhunt.* New York: Riverhead, 2020.

Leeson, Peter T. "An-*arrgh*-chy: The Law and Economics of Pirate Organization." *Journal of Political Economy* 115, no. 6 (2007): 1049–94.

Leeson, Peter T. *The Invisible Hook: The Hidden Economics of Pirates.* Princeton: Princeton University Press, 2009.

Meyer, W. R. "English Privateering in the War of the Spanish Succession, 1702–1713." *The Mariner's Mirror* 69, no.4 (1983): 435–46.

Rediker, Marcus. *Villains of All Nations: Atlantic Pirates in the Golden Age.* Boston: Beacon, 2004.

Tunstall, Brian, and Nicholas Tracy. *Naval Warfare in the Age of Sail: The Evolution of Fighting Tactics, 1650–1845.* New York: Wellfleet, 2001.

Woodard, Colin. *The Republic of Pirates: Being the True and Surprising Story of the Caribbean Pirates and the Man Who Brought Them Down.* Orlando, FL: Harcourt, 2007.

THE DONNER PARTY

Brown, Daniel James. *The Indifferent Stars Above: The Harrowing Saga of the Donner Party.* Boston: Mariner, 2009.

Diamond, Jared. "Living Through the Donner Party." *Discover Magazine,* January 18, 1992.

Dixon, Kelly J., et al. "'Men, Women, and Children Starving': Archaeology of the Donner Family Camp." *American Antiquity* 75, no. 3 (2010): 627–56.

Goodyear, Dana. "What Happened at Alder Creek." *The New Yorker,* April 24, 2006.

Grayson, Donald. "Donner Party Deaths: A Demographic Assessment." *Journal of Anthropological Research* 46, no. 3 (1990): 223–42.

Johnson, Kristin, ed. *"Unfortunate Emigrants": Narratives of the Donner Party*. Logan: Utah State University Press, 1996.

McLaughlin, Mark. *The Donner Party: Weathering the Storm*. Carnelian Bay, CA: Mic Mac Publishing, 2007.

Schutt, Bill. *Cannibalism: A Perfectly Natural History*. New York: Algonquin, 2017.

Stewart, George R. *Ordeal by Hunger: The Story of the Donner Party*. New York: Henry Holt, 1936.

THE 1906 EARTHQUAKE

"1906: The San Francisco Earthquake." *The New York Times*, April 19, 1906. Republished online March 12, 2011.

Borcherdt, Roger D., et al. "Prediction of Maximum Earthquake Intensity in the San Francisco Bay Region, California, for Large Earthquakes on the San Andreas and Hayward Faults." U.S. Geological Survey Miscellaneous Field Studies, Department of the Interior, 1977. Reprint published online August 10, 2009.

Ellsworth, William. "Earthquake History, 1769–1989." In *The San Andreas Fault System, California: U.S. Geological Survey Professional Paper 1515*, edited by Robert E. Wallace, 153–87. Washington, D.C.: U.S. Government Printing Office, 1990.

Fradkin, Philip L. *The Great Earthquake and Firestorms of 1906*. Berkeley: University of California Press, 2006.

Hansen, Gladys, and Emmet Condon. *Denial of Disaster: The Untold Story and Photographs of the San Francisco Earthquake and Fire of 1906*. Petaluma, CA: Cameron Books, 1989.

Lawson, Andrew C., and Harry F. Reid, eds. *The California Earthquake of April 18, 1906: Report of the State Earthquake Investigation Commission*. 2 vols. Washington, D.C.: Carnegie Institution, 1908.

Richardson, Robert D. *William James: In the Maelstrom of American Modernism*. Boston: Houghton Mifflin, 2006.

Robinson, Hadley. "Unraveling the Mystery of Mission Dolores." *Mission Local*, February 15, 2011.

Schmitz, E. E. "Proclamation by the Mayor Dated April 18, 1906." San Francisco, 1906. Available online at the Library of Congress: www.loc.gov/resource/rbpe.00202500/.

Thomas, Gordon, and Max Morgan-Witts. *The San Francisco Earthquake: A Minute-by-Minute Account of the 1906 Disaster.* New York: Stein and Day, 1971. Ebook: Open Road Integrated Media, 2014.

Tobriner, Stephen. "An EERI Reconnaissance Report: Damage to San Francisco in the 1906 Earthquake—A Centennial Perspective." *Earthquake Spectra* 22, no. 2, supplement (2006): 11–41.

Wallace-Wells, David. "The Return of the Urban Firestorm." *New York Magazine,* January 1, 2022.

Zoback, Mary Lou. "The 1906 Earthquake and a Century of Progress in Understanding Earthquakes and Their Hazards." *GSA Today* 16, nos. 4–5 (April/May 2006): 4–11.

THE SINKING OF THE *TITANIC*

Gleicher, David. *The Rescue of the Third Class on the Titanic: A Revisionist History.* Liverpool: Liverpool University Press, 2006.

Gleicher, David, and Lonnie Stevans. "Who Survived *Titanic*? A Logistic Regression Analysis." *International Journal of Maritime History* 16, no. 2 (2004): 61–93.

Hall, Wayne. "Social Class and Survival on the S.S. *Titanic*." *Social Science & Medicine 22, no. 6* (1986): 687–90.

Leighly, H. P., et al. "RMS *Titanic*: A Metallurgical Problem." *Journal of Failure Analysis and Prevention* 1, no. 2 (2001): 10–13.

Smith, Denis. "Exploring the Myth: The Sinking of the *Titanic*." *Industrial & Environmental Crisis Quarterly* 8, no. 3 (1994): 275–88.

Stettler, Jeffrey, and Brian Thomas. "Flooding and Structural Forensic Analysis of the Sinking of the RMS *Titanic*." *Ships and Offshore Structures* 8, nos. 3–4 (2013): 346–66.

Wilding, Edward. "Testimony: British Wreck Commissioner's Inquiry, Day 18." June 7, 1912. Available online at *Titanic* Inquiry Project, www.titanicinquiry.org/BOTInq/BOTInq18Wilding01.php.

THE WORST TORNADO IN AMERICAN HISTORY

Coleman, Timothy A., et al. "The History (and Future) of Tornado Warning Dissemination in the United States." *Bulletin of the American Meteorological Society* 95, no. 5 (2011): 567–82.

Dizikes, Peter. "When the Butterfly Effect Took Flight." *MIT Technology Review,* February 22, 2011.

Johns, Robert., et al. "The 1925 Tri-State Tornado Damage Path and Associated Storm System." *Electronic Journal of Severe Storms Meteorology* 8, no. 2 (2013): 1–33; Supplemental Material, c1—c31.

Larson, Erik. *Isaac's Storm: A Man, a Time, and the Deadliest Hurricane in History.* New York: Crown, 1999.

Lorenz, Edward N. "Predictability: Does the Flap of a Butterfly's Wings in Brazil Set Off a Tornado in Texas?" Paper presented before the American Association for the Advancement of Science, December 29, 1972.

Maddox, R. A., et al. "Meteorological Analyses of the Tri-State Tornado Event of March 1925." *Electronic Journal of Severe Storms Meteorology* 8, no. 1 (2013): 1–27.

Markowski, Paul, and Yvette Richardson. "What We Know and Don't Know About Tornado Formation." *Physics Today* 67, no. 9 (September 2014): 26.

Orf, Leigh, et al. "Evolution of a Long-Track Violent Tornado Within a Simulated Supercell." *Bulletin of the American Meteorological Society* 98, no. 1 (2017).

Rasmussen, Erik N., et al. "The Association of Significant Tornadoes with a Baroclinic Boundary on 2 June 1995." *Monthly Weather Review* 128, no. 1 (2000): 174–91.

"'Rebuild Murphysboro.' Pledge Redeemed." *The Daily Independent* (Murphysboro, IL), March 18, 1926.

Rotunno, Richard. "Supercell Thunderstorm Modeling and Theory." *In The Tornado: Its Structure, Dynamics, Prediction, and Hazards,* edited by C. Church et al., 57–73. Washington, D.C.: American Geophysical Union, 1993.